THE
INTENTIONAL DAD
EMBRACE AND FULFILL THE
PROMISE OF FATHERHOOD

THE
INTENTIONAL
DAD

EMBRACE AND FULFILL THE PROMISE OF FATHERHOOD

ARIC MANLY

Carpenter's Son Publishing

The Intentional Dad: Embrace and Fulfill the Promise of Fatherhood

Published by Carpenter's Son Publishing, Franklin, Tennessee

Published in association with Shane Crabtree of Christian Book Services, LLC
www.christianbookservices.com

Cover and Interior Design by Suzanne Lawing

Edited by Bob Irvin

Printed in the United States of America

978-1-954437-59-3

CONTENTS

Foreword   Growing Up as the Son of an
Intentional Dad 7

Before We Begin   11

Prologue   Invitation to Moms 13

Chapter One   The Promise of Fatherhood 23

Chapter Two   Generational Momentum 31

Chapter Three   Initiation: The Ancient Wisdom of
Intentional Fatherhood 43

Chapter Four   The Matrix 61

Chapter Five   And So It Begins 81

Chapter Six   Critical Weakness 101

Chapter Seven   Just Who Do You Think You Are? 115

Chapter Eight   Invitation 137

Chapter Nine   Vision 167

Chapter Ten   Purpose. 211

Next Steps   227

Appendix A   Knighthood Model for Initiation 231

Appendix B   Symbolism 251

Appendix C   Scripture for Further Exploration. 259

About the Author   263

Acknowledgments   265

Notes   269

Foreword
Ben Manly

GROWING UP AS THE SON
OF AN INTENTIONAL DAD

The other day I stumbled across a documentary titled *Dads*. It was a fantastic film celebrating men who have embraced the role of fatherhood. There was one question, however, that was presented to all the dads that caught my attention. They were all asked to finish the sentence: "A father is _____."

It's a challenging question! And it got me thinking about how I would answer it based on the vision of fatherhood that my dad has to share with you. I can't offer any firsthand experience for what fatherhood is like. What I can offer is insight into how a child might view their father, and what they need from him as they grow up. Which I think will be just as valuable.

* * *

I remember my days as a young boy being filled with bike rides around the neighborhood, construction of extravagant Thomas the Train tracks, and intense Nerf gun battles. And these things were always done with my "daddy." At that age, he was my playmate. All I wanted to do was play with him every day because my father was the one person in the world I wanted to be with most. Everything was made better when "Daddy" was part of it.

Once I entered elementary school, my definition of a father expanded. I had friends at school now that I could interact with to feed my desire for play. I still had a deep desire to play with my dad, but my heart needed something new from him as well. I needed to know that I was welcomed by him and that he wanted me to join him in his adventures. He and my uncles had several activities that I was now being invited into. I started to play golf with him. And, most importantly, he invited me into an epic journey toward my initiation.

The invitation he offered me is the crux of this book. It has been the single biggest factor in shaping my relationship with him and with my Abba. At such a young age I did not fully understand the importance of this invitation, but I leapt at the opportunity because he had chosen me.

What followed was a ten-year journey of spiritual development that taught me and my dad so much about ourselves, each other, and God. Sometimes we were on top of the world and sometimes we were at rock bottom. But we did it all together. At first, the journey was mostly about learning through observation and conversation with my dad. As time went on, my adventure became more demanding as I learned to take a more active role in my own growth and development. But I'm getting ahead of myself. At age 8 my scope of the world was still very small. My father was simply the most important person in the world, and he had invited me into an adventure with him. I could not feel more special.

* * *

As I entered my adolescent years, a new desire for my own adventures grew. I needed to test my limits and discover for myself the strength and courage I possessed. I remember family vacations to national parks and longing to explore the beauty that lay beyond the beaten path. I felt this pull toward the untamed in other areas during this phase too (sports, academics, getting a driver's license, talking to girls). All of it was important in discovering my capabilities as an adolescent.

The most fascinating thing for me during this stage, however, was watching how my peers approached this need at the same time. Most tested their capabilities, primarily by pushing away their parents. But I got the sense they were doing that out of bitterness instead of a healthy desire for independence. Many kids seemed to believe that wanting a close relationship with their parents was weak or immature. It was a lonely feeling knowing that I did want to be close with mine.

Knowing how a relationship between father and son was meant to be, it was hard for me to understand. My dad and I were able to avoid that unresolved strain in our relationship because we were committed to understanding ourselves and each other. In this phase of our journey, while I was testing my limits and capabilities, I needed my father to be my cheerleader. And he was my biggest fan.

As my initiation into manhood drew closer, we both knew my dad needed to gradually "let go of the seat," much like a dad teaching a kid to ride a bike for the first time. As he released me into the loving arms of the Father, his teaching, coaching, and guidance gradually gave way to cheering me on as I began to take all I had been learning and make it my own.

The process of initiation helped give me a deeply secure sense of identity and taught me how to have a deep, intimate relationship with my heavenly Father. I never had to wonder who I was as an adolescent because my dad worked hard to make the answer quite simple and relevant for me. I was a beloved son. Nothing more, nothing less. The longer I've walked this path, the more I understand that this was, and always has been, the greatest thing I could be. If my earthly father could confirm that identity in me, how much more could I receive it from my heavenly Father!

* * *

Now I am officially an adult, and a new phase of our relationship is emerging. I still deeply value my dad's company and advice. And I will always need him in the ways I have before. But now I can feel my heart needing something new from him again. Now I am beginning to see my father more and more as my *friend* . . . the way a friend should be. Someone who is willing to give tough love when I need it and a warm embrace just as willingly.

Parents say their kids grow up fast; I can believe that we do. Our relationship has grown and changed immensely over the years, and it hasn't always been the easiest to navigate. But we have always done it together. Through the causes for celebrations, times of sorrow, and everything between, we have savored it all as father and son.

* * *

I am so proud, then, to invite you to receive the clarity and insight my dad has gained through his experiences. I know what it meant to me growing up. I believe you and your family will also be blessed as you experience the joy of intentional fatherhood for yourselves.

BEFORE WE BEGIN

Let me start with a simple and heartfelt welcome. The fact that you have picked up a book called *The Intentional Dad* already says something about you. You are a man who is aware of his divine responsibility to his family, and you have a deep desire to lead your family well. In the pages ahead I share my fatherhood story with the hope that it will be an encouragement for you and your own fatherhood journey. Before turning to Chapter 1, I invite you to read the prologue, which is an invitation to moms. I wrote this book from one man to another, but the story I offer and invite you to discover for your family is one designed to be shared.

In my invitation to moms I explain the heart behind the story I share in this book, and this is an invitation I hope you come back to after you've finished. I share this at the start of the book to help men understand the backdrop for what I write before diving into the main part of the book. I also share this invitation at the beginning hoping it can support you, after you've finished reading, in communicating an invitation to the woman with whom you share this extraordinarily beautiful and sacred calling of parenthood.

I invite you into my heart behind my story—and then into the story itself. May God bless you and your family as you continue living out your sacred role as a father and husband.

Prologue

INVITATION TO MOMS

Let me start by simply saying thank you. You are a mom, and that is a sacred role, one to be honored and celebrated. It is challenging, tiring, and, many days, mundane and anonymous. So thank you for all you do every day to offer your tireless and sacrificial love to your kids and family.

Also, thank you for taking a few minutes to read this invitation. You are likely reading this because your husband asked you to. It may seem odd that he read (or is reading) a book titled *The Intentional Dad,* and now he wants to share it with you. If so, you are not the first to wonder what this may have to do with you.

The short answer is: a ton. Let me explain.

Yes, this book is written from one man to another as I share my story of healing and discovery with God and, specifically, how it has shaped my fatherhood journey with my kids and family. I am very aware that one of the unintended consequences of writing a book to dads is an understandable assumption from moms that it is not for them. I totally understand if you feel that way. So let me start there: I did write this book for your husband—but it was *not only* for him. What I share you will find extremely relevant for you, your family, and your sacred role and calling as a mother. It has never been my heart to exclude mothers and the critical and irreplaceable role you play in the great calling of parenthood you share with your husband. Far from it. I can tell you from experience that my wife's partnership, wisdom, strength, and support has been essential to the intentional work of initiation I describe throughout this book.

More than a decade ago I began a journey with God to understand my sacred role and divine responsibility of fatherhood. What I learned gave birth to a vision for my family to lead our kids through a ten-year process of initiation. It was a vision for a direction into something new and unique—at least in our culture. My wife was extremely supportive from the beginning but, at first, it was difficult for her to fully under-stand. That was, well, completely understandable. There was nobody else doing what we were trying to do . . . nobody we knew, anyway. So the only way forward was to simply do our best to follow where God was leading. At first that meant my wife would mostly observe my interactions with our kids as I tried to follow God's lead into the things he was helping me learn and understand. With time, though, she also began to see, and understand, the journey God had for our family.

It took us some time to understand and sort out what it looked like to share in this vision together. But we did. And when she found her place and her voice, it was like rocket fuel. It was such an important moment for us, and the indescribable joy we have known as a fami-ly simply would not have happened without her heart, strength, and wisdom as a wife and mother in partnership with me. We have been, and continue to be, an inseparable team, and it is no less important for you and your husband.

So let me explain why I wrote this book to and for men.

There are three very important reasons. I'll say up front that the ex-planations I offer involve exploring some things that, for some wom-en, are understandably sensitive issues. But I think you'll find that, even though they are potentially sensitive, what I have to say is not just another echo of what I believe to be tired and misguided perspectives on women and marriage. I ask only that you give me patience, and hear me out.

The first reason I wrote this book is a straightforward one. I am a man and a father. The story I share is, specifically, my story of fatherhood: a story I offer to other dads. I offer my experiences to men because I know the challenges, fears, and desires we men, as fathers, feel for our kids and families. So, yes, I am, first and foremost, going to relate to and offer my experiences most directly to men.

The second reason is that fatherhood is a sacred office—and it is very opposed. Don't get me wrong, motherhood is sacred as well. But as a father I am passionate about the daily assault men experience on their masculinity and fatherhood and the consequences these cause. Again, I very much understand that women are not at all immune from opposition, and they also experience daily assaults on their femininity and motherhood. In pointing out the challenges men face I am in no way minimizing anybody's experiences. I am simply saying that, as a man, I am in a position to speak to the opposition men face and to offer something we rarely get: encouragement and hope.

Masculinity, and fatherhood, are viciously opposed, and the impact on men and their hearts is having a devastating effect on you and your kids. It really isn't a difficult thing to observe. Masculinity is increasingly seen as dangerous, predatory, domineering, and selfish. Rarely, if ever, are men celebrated as good, much less essential, to the well-being of their families and the world in general. The shaming is so prominent that many men, trying to find refuge, simply withdraw and disengage; they don't really know what else is left to do. The consequences of this trend aren't just to the men driven to disengagement and passivity. It adds to the assault you feel as a wife and mother as you bear more and more of the burden of caring for your kids and family. It is a horrible cycle that simply must, and can, be broken. It is a cycle that is broken through the encouragement, hope, understanding, and healing we all so desperately need. This is what I hope to offer in sharing my story with other men.

The third and most important reason lies in my desire to honor what I believe to be God's design for marriage and parenthood. I am talking about God's design for men to lead. Now, before you throw the book aside, please hear me when I say that I understand if you are skeptical or wary just at the very mention of these things. There is a ton of baggage here, and much harm has been done in the name of "honoring God's word." So I get that women—and rightfully so—have no tolerance for tired and demeaning "norms" that would have you believe Scripture is "clear" about gender roles in marriage—conveniently, "norms" that would have you sacrifice your dignity, strength, and individuality. I join you in rejecting such ideas.

Now, even with that said, I do believe it is part of God's design for men to lead their families. So let me explain a bit more about what I believe to be a much more accurate understanding of the design God has provided, and I seek to honor.

All right. Time for a little theology.

Let's start with the elephant in the room. The verse. Yep. That one.

> *Wives, submit yourselves to your own husbands*
> *as you do to the Lord* (Ephesians 5:22).

There it is. That word. *Submit.*

Okay, we've said it. It's on the table. That one verse has been so abused, misused, and, in my not so humble opinion, so badly misunderstood that it is very, very difficult to recover what I think to be one of the most beautiful and hopeful pictures in all of Scripture for what God intends for marriage. So I know it is a lot to ask for some women to take a closer look at something that has been so painful. I *am*, though, asking you to do just that. Something I find to be an extremely helpful exercise is the idea of "extracting the precious from the worthless." This is an idea that comes from the words of the prophet Jeremiah. I explain it more in the book, but let's take a short look here.

Let's start with that word, submit, itself. Often it's helpful to just go back to the clear definition. You will find this in Merriam-Webster:

Submit (verb): accept or yield to a superior force
or to the authority of another person[1]

Taken by itself, it would seem that Paul is telling the Ephesian women to submit to their husbands as superior authority figures. But did you see the one bad word in that sentence? (Superior.) I think there are several reasons we can dismiss this idea. At the top of the list is the verse directly before Ephesians 5:22

Submit to <u>one another</u> out of reverence for Christ
(Ephesians 5:21; <u>my emphasis</u> added).

That, well . . . changes things. Before he addresses the women, Paul talks to the men and the women *together*, telling them that God's design for marriage lies in submission—*equal submission*—to one another. In other words, in telling both men and women to submit to one another, he is pointing out what should be obvious: each, as a son or daughter of God, and made in His image, carries an inherent authority. The married life, then, is a mutual submission to and honoring of the inherent human dignity each carries as an image bearer of God. So with that one verse some misconceptions begin to clear up. The problem may not be with the idea of submission after all! The problem may be that, in misunderstanding the design of *mutual* submission, we have been fighting, resisting, and undermining something extraordinary.

Which leads me back to Merriam-Webster. This time, in the thesaurus, we find antonyms for the word submit like fight and resist.[2] In other words, maybe there's another, perhaps more subtle way of understanding submit: acceptance of what you had once been fighting and resisting.

Paul is writing to people who are trying to figure out what it means to live as followers of Jesus. They were unlearning old assumptions and relearning life by God's design (i.e., submitting to God—just as we are learning to do). As the unlearning and relearning turns to the topic of marriage, Paul starts with the idea of submission. Why? Because it is an incredibly powerful idea that, properly understood, would help them leave behind the demeaning and broken framework of marriage as they had been living it in their culture. Namely, we are talking about a first-century society in which men enjoyed social status, respect, and honor far beyond women. So for Paul to use the word *submit* was, actually, quite radical because he is telling his readers to turn from the old way—to stop resisting God's design and, instead, submit to one another as *equals*. That was a radical idea then—and it is no less revolutionary and hopeful for us today! What, then, does that submission look like?

More extracting is helpful here. First, yes, there is a yielding to authority, but not like we might be thinking. Paul challenges both men *and* women to stop resisting God's vision for marriage when he tells women to submit in the same way the church (read: men and women of God's family) submits to Christ. Yes, he specifically tells women to submit, but not in a one-sided, demeaning sacrifice of dignity. Instead, he tells them: submit in the same way you are learning to submit to Jesus' authority in your life. And knowing Jesus' true heart for us, we know that submitting to him is never a demeaning sacrifice of dignity. Quite the opposite. That, again, changes things.

The context for submission, then—what was radical and new—was the vision for what they were submitting to: "authority" as modeled by Christ. Specifically, that would be a model of sacrificial love that honors, serves, liberates, and *elevates a man's wife above himself.* Having given the women a new and hopeful picture for God's design, Paul turns to the men to explain God's design for them in marriage.

He gives them an incredibly lofty standard: to be a man who loves and leads his family in the same way Jesus loves and leads. To love and honor her as Jesus loves and honors her. And how did Jesus love and honor her?

Yeah.

He died for her.

So it's not just that Paul was telling men to treat women as equals—he actually took it much further. He tells them God's design is for men to elevate their wives in word and deed above themselves—the same way Jesus loves us!

Putting it all together, then, an inspiring picture emerges—a beautiful dance of mutual respect, honor, and sacrificial love. A man offers his heart, his life, and his leadership in intentional, devoted, sacrificial love and service to his wife. A woman receives what her husband offers and, in so doing, breathes life into it as she offers her heart, life, and leadership in intentional, devoted, sacrificial love back to her husband. *He receives that life and honors his wife as he then offers the fruit of mutual submission and sacrificial love back to her.* It is life-giving, honoring, and stunningly beautiful—a dance God intends for you and your husband. A design to live in oneness and to thrive together.

This is the design I want to honor: God's design for your husband's masculine heart and his God-given desires to lead and love well as a husband and father. Our modern culture has, in many ways, swung in the opposite direction of that first-century culture. Shame, contempt, disdain, and mistrust are rampant and, for many men, have them retreating in disengagement and passivity. So, in honoring God's design, I want to offer encouragement, understanding, hope, and clarity that will help him find his strength again. A man's desire to lead is a God-given desire, and the world needs men to be restored to that desire. This starts with you and your family. He was made to lead, and the leadership he offers to you now is not characterized by what he wants *from* you but what he wants for you and your family. It is not characterized by *demand* but by *invitation*.

Which brings me back to what all this has to do with you.

In this book I share my story of fatherhood. I offer what I have learned and experienced through more than ten years of living out a journey of intentional fatherhood with my kids—and my wife. I do not have the words to adequately describe the joy we have known as a family, a joy I very much want for you, your husband, and your kids.

You have read this invitation, likely, because of your husband's desire to lead and love well. It is a desire he has been carrying with him—again, likely very quietly. He has known what he longs for but has struggled to truly understand what it looks like to embrace and fulfill his divine responsibility as a father and husband. He has longed for clarity and, for some time, done his best to love and lead without it. But that is changing.

This journey he has begun he now offers to you. The dance continues as you receive his invitation. I do not presume to have addressed everything that might be relevant to you as a woman, wife, and mother. But as you receive your husband's invitation, I believe you'll find this book to be extremely relevant, and precious, for you as well. You will begin a journey of healing and redemption of your own heart. As you do, together you and your husband will nurture a shared vision for embracing and fulfilling your sacred roles as parents.

So, yes, I wrote to your husband. But with each page of the manuscript, I had mothers like you very much in mind. The journey your husband is inviting you into is a journey meant for you to take together: an ongoing dance of offering and receiving the beauty, strength, wisdom, understanding, insight, personality, and gifting each of you has to offer. It is a fiercely intentional love that, together, in intimate partnership with God, you will offer to your kids.

From the beginning it has always been my hope that I could share my story with other men, that they could see and understand their calling to fatherhood, and, in doing so, invite their wives on a shared journey of intentional parenthood. It is an invitation I extend alongside your husband, and one I offer in hopeful anticipation of what God has in store for you, your husband, and your family.

May God bless you and your family richly as you receive the invitation and continue the dance.

Chapter One

THE PROMISE OF FATHERHOOD

Children are a heritage from the Lord, offspring a reward from him.
Like arrows in the hands of a warrior are children born in one's youth.
Blessed is the man whose quiver is full of them (Psalm 127:3-5).

It was a stormy day in April. But the weather hardly mattered in that moment. In fact, almost nothing felt important compared to what I was witnessing and experiencing. It was surreal, magical, divine . . . sacred, really. My wife was giving birth to our first child. The moment was bathed in anticipation as, over nine months, she and I had been experiencing the awe of his development in the womb. Early on we had signed up for an email subscription that delivered to our inbox a weekly update on his approximate size (cleverly done by comparing his size, usually, with a vegetable—suddenly peas and lima beans became very very interesting items) and what parts of his body were developing. The words "fearfully and wonderfully made" and "knit together in my mother's womb" took on an entirely new depth of significance. And with each passing day, the anticipation grew for the day he would take his first breath and we could look into the eyes of this beautiful child.

Moments before, Mary Jo and I were playing Yahtzee to pass the time, but we never finished because she rather suddenly stopped playing . . . and talking . . . and moving. Only slow breathing. The rest is a blur. The team of doctors and nurses swept into action. At first I was at her side and we did that breathing thing we learned to do. But at some point, that was no longer necessary. My job was done, and all that was left for me was to watch it all unfold.

Time seemed to stop. The buzz around the room and the urgency of the medical team all seemed to go silent. Everything felt like it was in slow motion as I breathed in the divine moment. My son emerged and looked straight at me. I looked deeply into his eyes, mine full of tears, and simply said "Hi!" He blinked a couple times, and then came that beautiful sound as he breathed in to let out a small cry. I don't know how I stayed on my feet. The best way I can describe that moment was that the veil between eternity and this world was pulled back and I had witnessed something divine. My wife and I loved this little boy long before he was born. But in that moment, something was awakened in me—and I would never be the same. As I looked into my son's eyes, the weight of the moment struck me deeply as the anticipation of those nine months culminated in that precious moment . . . I was a dad. I had a divine responsibility to that little boy, and my desire to live up to that promise was fully alive. All at once, the promise of fatherhood was something hopeful, inspiring, beautiful—and terrifying.

I didn't have a moment of sleep that first night as I held my son, literally, all night.

That was how my fatherhood journey began. Maybe you can relate to my experience or, quite possibly, the dawn of your fatherhood journey was nothing like mine. Some of you were there for the birth of your child, but "divine" is the last word you would use to describe the moment. Some of you weren't in the room at all. Still others are fathers to children who are not flesh and blood but no less your sons and daughters—through adoption, fostering, or as stepchildren. While the dawn of our fatherhood journeys may be unique (or perhaps yours has yet to begin), if you're reading this book it is highly likely we all have something in common. We all share a deep sense of the hopeful, inspiring, beautiful, and sacred role of fatherhood—as well as the fear connected to the divine responsibility we all feel for the children we love so deeply.

And really, do we need to make the case for the significance of fatherhood? We could just start with Solomon's words from Psalm 127. The man whose name is synonymous with wisdom calls children a "heritage" and "reward" meant as a blessing from God. And what man, including our heavenly Father, doesn't beam with joy as his children call out to him, "Daddy!" Fatherhood is from God. It is, in my not so humble opinion, the most important work he has ordained for men. Put simply, the world needs men to be fathers. It is clearly a significant part of God's design for the planet.

Instinctively, I think, most men know this. The world certainly knows this. Unfortunately, though, the world knows it more and more by the absence of fathers. The purpose of this book, however, is not to be another voice of shame for men. There are plenty of those voices—and none of them are at all helpful. But suffice it to say, this is not hard to see: when men neglect their divine responsibility, the effect is devastating. Where fathers are absent, poverty is far more likely, drug and alcohol abuse increases, academic achievement declines, physical and emotional health suffer, and crime increases.[1] So even in the absence of men embracing their divine responsibilities, we see just how sacred their role is.

Fatherhood is a gift from God. It should come as no surprise that such a sacred office would be opposed. I am talking about opposition from an enemy who Jesus teaches is the "father of lies" and whose sole purpose is to steal, kill, and destroy. Knowing just how important fatherhood is, it is no wonder that our enemy would be working to do just that: steal, kill, and destroy fatherhood.

Back to my fatherhood story. The day my first child was born awakened something deep inside me. My father's heart was more alive and aware than it had ever been. But back then, I was unaware and unprepared for a ruthless and determined enemy on the prowl. Slowly but surely, the false promises of career, title, and achievement had a numbing effect on my father's heart. Without realizing it, the hope of validation in those things slowly became more important to me than being a dad. The enemy had lured me onto a path of destruction and stolen something precious from me and my family. It would take a major shake-up to get me to see it. That is a story I will share in the pages ahead. For now, let's just say that the shake-up would come, and it was a painful experience. After years of searching for significance in doing "important" and "impressive" things, the piercing words of a faithful friend made clear what I had lost. This book is my story of rescue in the midst of failure and brokenness—a rescue that would lead to healing and a restoration of all the hope, inspiration, and beauty of my sacred role of fatherhood that had once been so clear to me on that stormy April evening.

> Slowly but surely, the false promises of career, title, and achievement had a numbing effect on my father's heart.

I suspect something similar is what compelled you to pick up this book. Like me, something in you has been awakened. You already know how important fatherhood is. Good dads are deeply aware of their divine responsibilities to their kids and family. But for so many good men, along with that awareness, they secretly carry a heavy burden. Every day they are offering the best of their good father's heart for their family, but in spite of that they are haunted by the fear that it isn't and never will be enough. I know, because I lived under the shadow of that fear as well. If you know that burden, if you secretly fear that your fatherhood journey is destined to end in failure and regret, there is hope.

The problem is not you or your heart. The problem for countless good men like you is simply that you lack the clarity of God's design for fatherhood. So good men like you have done exactly what you would expect. You have done your best to fulfill your sacred role, but if you're being honest, to this point you have simply been taking your best guess at what it means to do that. However, fatherhood feels way too important to be left to your "best guess." Yet what else could you do? Where could you turn? Who could teach you? Believe me, I know the weight of that burden. This book is my story of God inviting me into that same fear. It was a journey into things I did not expect—a story of rescue and discovery I now share with you.

God *does* have a great deal to say about fatherhood. It is something he very much intends for us men to know and understand. What I learned, and what we have experienced and continue to experience as a family for well over a decade, is what I offer to you here.

There is a design for fatherhood, and you can learn it.

However, it may not be what you expect. What I offer is an invitation to share in my story and, at the same time, to set out on a journey of your own. There are some things, I suspect, that will be new, unique, and maybe even seem odd to you. Some of you will find parts of this difficult, and you may even wonder at times if it is necessary. That's okay. I understand those thoughts. I had many of them myself as God led me into new, unique, and sometimes seemingly odd things. I simply ask that you hear me out—and try for yourself the things God has taught me through the years. Yes, some of it will be challenging. I can also assure you, it is worth it.

I am now a father of three children. What I share is born of my own desire for clarity and understanding for my sacred role with my children. Over time God met my desire, and we began living into that clarity and understanding beginning when my oldest son was 8. A decade later, that journey culminated in one of the most joyful and emotional experiences of my life as his mother and I initiated him into manhood with a powerful and memorable ceremony to seal the moment. It was a joy for our family that I cannot come close to describing—a joy I very deeply long for you and your family to know as well.

But the story is far from over. It continues for my daughter, who will soon be initiated into womanhood, and my youngest son, whose initiation journey officially began the same weekend we initiated my oldest son.

And now it continues with you.

But this book isn't just for men with young children. Fatherhood is a calling we men share, and it is precious no matter where you are on that journey. Some of you may have picked up this book before your fatherhood journey has even begun. It is an outpouring of your good heart that you are already awakened to the calling of fatherhood and long to understand it even before your children are born.

Or perhaps your journey is further along and your kids are older now, your years of primary influence already largely behind you. Maybe you are starting to experience what way too many dads experience: regret and failure. Your relationship with your kids is okay, but deep down you are beginning to feel the cold breath of regret with a nagging sense that you may have been missing something. Or, worse, your relationship with your kids is becoming cold and distant, maybe even strained. Your wife is frustrated with you, and the messages of shame are starting to feel true. You are beat up, discouraged, almost defeated. Still, here you are, refusing to give up and compelled by your good father's heart to offer something precious to your kids and family.

Finally, there are those whose children are grown and the pain of regret and failure seem to be the final word of your fatherhood journey. But you are here as an act of holy defiance, refusing to accept a lie from the same enemy who destroyed what you had in the first place. He's been working to keep you locked in despair. But your courage and resolve have kept you going. Your journey is *not* done. You have so much to offer.

Wherever you are, I want to offer you something we dads don't get too often: encouragement and hope. The world needs men to step into their sacred role of fatherhood with confidence, clarity, and understanding. However, the story of regret and failure is so common that, I'm afraid, it becomes hard for a man to envision even moderate success. Doesn't it make sense, though, that something as important as fatherhood is a role we men were made to flourish in? More than that, no matter where you are in your fatherhood journey, this is something you can experience. You are giving the best of what you know to give. But something inside is unsettled. You've been living with that secret burden—an ever present threat of regret and failure haunts you. Well, failure and regret are *not* inevitable, nor do they have the final word for you. There is hope. There is a design for fatherhood. You can understand it and learn it. You *can* flourish as a dad for your children and your family, again, no matter where you are. But just as I had to do, you must venture back into your own heart. Healing, wholeness, and redemption are still available for the courageous men who will follow God into the unknown.

> Healing, wholeness, and redemption are still available for the courageous men who will follow God into the unknown.

Men, you were made for many things . . . but there is nothing more sacred than your role as fathers. This book is an invitation for men—

men just like you—to embrace and fulfill the promise of fatherhood. Your heart was made to be alive to that promise. Awaken to it again. It is time for you to rekindle hope and embrace your sacred role. All that seemed possible once can be realized. You can foster intimacy with your children, faithfully shepherd your kids through the ups and downs of life, and bestow a deep sense of identity as beloved sons and daughters of God—and initiate them into adulthood, knowing with joy and pride that they are living lives of intimate apprenticeship with him.

That is the promise you were meant to fulfill. Now that something is stirring within you, the real work can begin. The journey of a thousand miles indeed begins with a single step.

Onward!

Next: Fatherhood is a gift from God given to us men. It is indeed sacred—and it is opposed.

Chapter Two

GENERATIONAL MOMENTUM

Do not bow down to any idol or worship it, because I am the Lord your
God and I tolerate no rivals. I bring punishment on those who hate me
and on their descendants down to the third and fourth generation. But
I show my love to thousands of generations of those who love me and
obey my laws (Exodus 20:5, 6, GNT).

I love to golf. Well, usually. No golfer has a purely romantic relationship with the game. It can be cruel and unfair. There are times when I
play that I can do everything right, strike the ball perfectly, and look
up only to see the one overhanging branch no more than two inches
thick knock it sideways into the water on the other side of the fairway.

I have played the game most of my life. That, itself, is a minor mir-
acle because most of those years I had very little reason to love the
game. You see, the vast majority of those years, I suffered from the
bane of amateur golfers everywhere: the slice. Mine was legendary. I
got used to watching that wild curve to the right and climbing through
weeds and woods in search of errant shots. Occasionally I would ac-

tually get to hit a ball from the fairway, but rarely was it the fairway of the hole I was playing! Still, I played. I suppose there were just enough good shots to keep me going, and when they did happen, I really had no idea why. And I certainly didn't know how to repeat that rare shot. Believe me, I tried to figure it out. I always had plenty of advice, and since I was so desperate to figure it out, I was eager to try just about anything. This elbow in, that wrist out, one leg forward, one leg back, back swing here, follow through there . . . grip adjustments, stance adjustments, aim adjustments. None of it mattered. In essence, I was trying a whole bunch of different things—and changing nothing.

There is an old saying I'm sure you've heard: insanity is doing the same thing over and over and expecting a different result. Which is exactly what I was doing. For years. Each new round started with the promise of deliverance from my torment. And each round would end with the same despair. Even though I thought I was trying different things, the truth is that none of it changed things where they mattered. So the slice never went away. Until . . . I finally came to the conclusion that I needed help. And not from the other amateurs from whom I'd been getting advice. No, I realized the kind of help I needed was from someone who could actually help me understand exactly what was faulty about my swing and teach me how to correct it.

Guess what? It worked! I finally found an instructor who could do those things for me. For the first time in my life, I truly did understand what caused my problems and, therefore, how to fix them. Now, years of repetition of doing the wrong thing doesn't just disappear over-night. I would hit many more slices. But the difference was I knew what caused those wayward shots and what I needed to do to fix them. Finally, after years of going nowhere, I slowly began to get better. Oh, I'm still very much an amateur. But when I play now, I have far more good shots than bad.

The turning point was the moment I finally decided I needed help, and I sought that help from someone who could actually offer it.

What does this have to do with fatherhood? Great question. Bear with me; I'll get right back to that. First, let me share another story. This one is fiction, but the truths explored in the story are hardly fictional. Years ago, Disney made a movie, starring Bruce Willis, called *The Kid*. It is the story of Russell Duritz, a driven, shallow, narcissistic man who has built a successful career as an image consultant for high-powered entertainment, political, and journalism professionals. But for all his success professionally, he is an abject failure as a human being. He is cruel, selfish, impatient, and . . . alone. Surprisingly, his rescue comes in the form of his 8-year-old self—on his 40th birthday. The young Russ and the adult Russ find themselves brought together in a cosmic twist. And through that encounter, adult Russ is forced to understand his past and how key moments in his young life set him on a path to become the man he became.

That is the backdrop to what, for me, is the most impactful scene of the movie. As the story unfolds, we learn Russ's story and about one moment, in particular, that cemented his course. As an 8-year-old, Russ is a paunchy, awkward kid who gets picked on at school and is largely ignored by his dad. On one fateful day at school, he got in trouble with one of his tormentors. His mom took the call and made her way to school to pick up Russ. The scene picks up with Russ and his mom having just arrived home. They are still standing on the front walkway as Russell's dad gets home. His dad quickly rushes to usher his wife indoors and, a short time later, emerges again through the front door in a rage. His words are like daggers to a young boy's heart as he berates his son for causing so much trouble. They are devastating: "Are you trying to kill her faster?" In that moment Russell learns for the first time that his mother is dying and, of course, he begins to cry. Again, his father strikes another withering blow to his young son as he wipes his tears and commands him to stop crying . . . now. He finishes the moment with one more dagger as he walks away, saying, "Grow up."

In the first chapter I briefly described a day when God used my friend's piercing words to shake me up. A journey began to find healing for a heart I knew was in desperate need of care. A big part of that healing came as I began to understand the importance of exploring my past so that I could, like Russ Duritz, understand key moments that were impacting who I had become. For the first time in my life, I really started to look deeply into the ways I had been wounded and the things I came to believe because of those wounds. For me, this hit me doubly hard as a man who had been reawakened to his divine responsibility of fatherhood. I was, for the first time, coming to terms with my own past, especially wounds born of my relationship with my own dad. At the same time I was confronting, for the first time, the devastating thought that I was wounding my own children. Frankly, it all felt overwhelming. Was it inevitable that I would continue a legacy of wounding from father to son, father to daughter? Was it inevitable that my fatherhood journey was going to be a story of failure and regret? At the time, that thought scared me—deeply. It was the deepening of a heart cry that had started to grow before but, in that moment, became desperate. My children were still young, so, I thought to myself, *At least I have a chance at a different story.* And it was a story I now wanted very badly to be different.

Here again, I have to pause. I'm afraid that if I don't say more, there is way too much room for shame and misunderstanding that could steal from what I most want to share. If I say nothing more, too many men, including my own dad, would rightly conclude that this is, in fact, a critique on their failures. But I bring up the difficult topic of father wounds not to lash out at my father or yours. The reality is that no one is perfect. All of us dads have failed our kids. So, no, this is not a shaming over our failures. After all, we're all in the same boat. But that doesn't mean we should ignore those failures either, because there is an impact, and it is more significant than you may realize. There is a ripple effect of our failures that carries from generation to generation.

Yes, in my own journey into these heart issues, the healing and restoration I have enjoyed simply could not have happened without a clear-eyed look at some moments that had a profound and lasting impact on my heart and life. That journey did open the door to some extremely deep emotions, some that would last for years. Yes, my dad wounded me. I hate that he may be one of many men to read this. No father enjoys hearing that. And this son does not enjoy saying it. I don't like the thought that this topic is hurting him. I love him, respect him, and am so grateful for so many wonderful things he offered me as well. But here's the thing: there is no sugarcoating or ignoring that he did also wound me, and I simply could not have had the healing my heart so desperately needed without taking Jesus' invitation to go into those moments, understand them, and allow him to heal them.

There are things we were made to need and want from our dads. This is such a painful—and for some, taboo—subject because the reality is, each and every one of us has experienced this. We didn't get what we needed. For some of you, wounds of abuse, abandonment, or adultery (among other things) have been obvious, and devastating. For others, the wounds are maybe less obvious, but the impact to your heart and story are also profoundly significant and never should be minimized. For some, to go back into your story feels too overwhelming and painful, and for many of us, it feels dishonoring to admit the wounding, much less walk deeply into it. I could have simply gone on with my life ignoring the truth of moments that my dad failed me. Maybe, in some ways, that would have been easier—in the short term, anyway. But I also never would have come to the gift that is wrapped within that pain: the compassion of a God who grieves with us over what our fathers failed to give, and an invitation for us to let him be all that our earthly father was not. And, maybe most importantly of all, to begin to see God more and more as he is, independent of my earthly father.

One thing that has been so helpful for me in all of this is some perspective. Here is the thing about my dad and yours. His dad hurt him. And how about his dad? Yep, broken. It doesn't take long to see a much bigger picture. Fatherhood has been a broken institution all the way back to Adam. Men, we've all been swept up in it: a generational momentum of broken fatherhood. That is not a truth intended to minimize or dismiss your individual experience. It has helped me, though, realize just how desperate we all are for rescue.

And that is the very thing Jesus is inviting us to receive every day.

Which is exactly what the passage from Exodus atop this chapter alludes to. I know the language of those verses is, well, hard. "Tolerate no rivals"? Bring "punishment on those who hate me"? "To the third and fourth generation"? Those are some rather intimidating words, and they raise some tough questions. Perhaps the most difficult question for me is the idea that children are "punished" for the way their parents (ancestors) missed the mark. That just doesn't seem right and, honestly, feels petty. Which, I think, is a clue that perhaps we should keep working to understand. Are there other parts of Scripture that talk about ancestors, sin, and punishment? As it turns out, yes. Let's look at one:

> *A son is not to suffer because of his father's sins, nor a father because of the sins of his son* (Ezekiel 18:20, GNT).

Okay. So this seems a direct contradiction of what God says in Exodus. Curious. But let's keep exploring. Perhaps this exchange between Jesus and his disciples will tell us more:

> *Walking down the street, Jesus saw a man blind from birth. His disciples asked, "Rabbi, who sinned: this man or his parents, causing him to be born blind?" Jesus said, "You're asking the wrong question. You're looking for someone to blame.*

*There is no such cause-effect here. Look instead for
what God can do"* (John 9:1-5, The Message).

The question the disciples ask is revealing. They saw the blind man's condition and immediately assumed it was punishment for sin. As God's word in Exodus would seem to indicate, the disciples concluded that the man's blindness was a punishment from God either for the man's sin or that of his parents. But Jesus blew up that premise. Sometimes there is cause and effect, and there are consequences directly related to our failures. But in this instance, Jesus reveals that things are far more complicated. We want to blame. Instead, Jesus says, "Look for what God can do." With that in mind, let's look again at Exodus.

God does say he will bring punishment on those who hate him—and on those within that line down to the third and fourth generation. But he says more. He says he will show love to thousands of generations of those who love and obey him. So let's take Jesus at his word and, instead, look for what God is telling us about what he is doing. Could it be that the primary concern is not so much about punishment and reward as it is the issue of hating and loving? Specifically, the hate and love of concern here is our hate or love of God. To hate God is to choose disobedience—a rival, an alternative way of living outside of his design for us. And that design is to live out of intimate connection with and trust in him. To love God is to choose his way and his design for us and, yes, there are consequences for these options. The punishment, then, is God simply allowing the natural consequences of choosing our own way to unfold. Those consequences are not insignificant. There are some consequences that have a ripple effect from generation to generation. As long as the "hating of God" continues, so does the ripple effect.

This is the issue of generational momentum.

Doesn't that ring true? Look at the ugliness of human brokenness: divorce, murder, addiction, abuse, passivity, bigotry, callousness, depression, entitlement—and observe how these issues perpetuate from generation to generation. Our attempts to "fix" these problems are, frankly, no different than my feeble attempts to follow all the free advice I received to "fix" my very bad golf slice. All of it amounted to nothing more than superficial changes that never came close to helping me truly understand the problem and actually fix it.

Men, when it comes to fatherhood, I hope you are beginning to see what we are all up against. There is a generational momentum that has been sweeping all of us along.

Frankly, we've all been more or less taking stabs in the dark . . . making our best guesses . . . when it comes to fatherhood. Like all the "advice" I would get for my golf swing, we've been trying a whole bunch of stuff but never really understanding what has been broken or how to fix it. Really, men, what is—or has been—your plan for fatherhood? Let me take a crack at it. You started with the things you liked about your childhood (if there was anything) and kept those things. Then you determined the things you didn't like and vowed to eliminate those things. Voilà! A plan. I know, I know. That sounds harsh. Once again, though, I do not offer this observation in shame. The reality is: what else were we going to do? It's not like other options and resources were abundant—at least that we knew of. You didn't know a better way because your dad never taught you . . . and his dad never taught him . . . and so on. So, again, I can totally relate to the dilemma because that is exactly where I was before encountering the movie scene with Russ Duritz.

Let's go back to the rest of what God had to say in Exodus. Namely, he is eager to abundantly and lavishly pour out his love—to a thousand generations of those who love him or, put another way, choose him and his ways. Wow! He just cannot wait for us to get to the point where we realize how feeble and consequential "our way" has been and awaken to our desire to learn his design for living, for fatherhood. This is not a petty, vengeful Father. No, this is a Father who loves his children deeply and wants the best for us. Even if we must learn that for ourselves the hard way.

My story had come to a turning point. I was finally ready to admit I needed help. I could see that my "plan" was only going to perpetuate the unredeemed brokenness and wounding from my childhood—and that my dad had experienced in his. I needed to go to someone who could help me understand fatherhood as it was intended and, not only that, learn how to bring that type of loving leadership to my family.

It is one thing to learn the proper technique of a golf swing; there are many good coaches and teachers out there. Fathering, though? Well, there was only one place I was going to go for that: the author of fatherhood himself. So now my whole being turned desperately to him. I had been awakened to my sacred role, and now I could see clearly what I was up against. No longer was I content to be swept along in generational momentum. So I drove a stake in the ground and decided it was time for me to take a stand against the current. I wanted to understand God's design for fatherhood. My heart was crying out to God for clarity and an eager, desperate search began. For well more than a year, God let me sit with that desperation. I read, prayed, studied, and listened. A lot. What I didn't know then, but clearly understand now, is his wisdom in making me wait—and work.

For the first time in my life I was learning to be fathered as a beloved son. I now know this fundamental truth to be the cornerstone for everything else I would learn. The day would come when he would answer my prayer. But it was something I needed to grow into. I wanted to offer all I could to my kids and family. But I simply would not be able to give what I didn't have. So first I had to learn what it was to be fathered. To begin living, for the first time, as God's beloved son. From there I would learn how to father my children.

So, men, you too are invited to take a stand and drive a stake in the ground. This issue of generational momentum has been impacting all of us, and wrapped in your story are very specific ways things have played out from generation to generation in your family. Perhaps you never knew affection with your dad. I'm betting it's hard for you to be affectionate with your children. Maybe your dad made it clear that emotions and manhood don't go together. Chances are your children are now learning that from you. Maybe your dad was distant and passive. It's likely you are too. Perhaps you grew up in a broken family. I'm betting several of those issues are at work in your family. Or, for some of you, generational momentum has been generated through your determination to not be like your dad. He was passive; you are involved, but also unaware of how that might still be wounding to your kids. He was a disciplinarian; you rarely correct and discipline your kids. The point is that without truly understanding, our "best guesses" never get to the core issues. We're trying everything, understanding nothing, and, therefore, still hitting that bad "slice." I'll say it again because it is so important: none of this is offered in the spirit of condemnation. Instead, I hope you see it as an invitation. Not mine. God's.

"Come to me, all of you who are tired from carrying heavy loads, and I will give you rest" (Matthew 11:28, GNT).

"Come to me." Jesus is offering each of us an invitation. There is hope in the face of generational momentum. There is a design for fatherhood. You can learn it, and you can bring it to your family. It will not necessarily be easy. And, to be clear, I am not trying to imply that this is a path to perfect fatherhood. Far from it. It has been well more than a decade since I drove that stake in the ground, but I have not been spared failure and wounding. I am a man, like you, who is broken and imperfect and, like any other man, I have moments in which I fail and hurt my children. But as I've grown and learned how to live into God's design, the result has been that grace, understanding, redemption, love, and joy have all grown out of my weakness and brokenness—things I know God wants every father to experience with his family. Yes, I've hurt my kids. But some of my most cherished moments with them are when we've grieved those failures together, picked each other up, dusted each other off, and continued walking together with God into the promise of fatherhood.

Driving a stake in the ground against generational momentum, turning away from your "best guess" plan for fatherhood and toward God's design . . . these steps will not magically change things for you and your family overnight. Instead, like fixing a slice, they are the *beginning* of a process of unlearning and relearning. It will take courage, persistence, and perseverance. It will be opposed and, maybe, at times, it will feel like nothing's happening. But with time you will begin to realize for yourself and your family the promise of fatherhood.

And "thousands of generations" will never be the same.

Next: Standing against the current of generational momentum is taking a stand against the current of your own family history—but it is also taking a cultural stand.

Chapter Three

INITIATION: THE ANCIENT WISDOM OF INTENTIONAL FATHERHOOD

I know what it means to lack, and I know what it means to experience overwhelming abundance. For I'm trained in the secret of overcoming all things, whether in fullness or in hunger. And I find that the strength of Christ's explosive power infuses me to conquer every difficulty (Philippians 4:12, 13, The Passion Translation).

If people can't see what God is doing, they stumble all over themselves; But when they attend to what he reveals, they are most blessed (Proverbs 29:18, The Message).

Define yourself radically as one beloved by God. God's love for you and his choice of you constitute your worth. Accept that, and let it become the most important thing in your life. —Brennan Manning[1]

The Beast. That is what we called my first car. It was a '77 Monte Carlo, and it had more in common with a tank than a car. It was huge, and it was ugly. It was a primer gray with rust accents, torn and faded red interior, an AM radio, four balding tires, and two huge doors (though only the passenger's side actually opened). My parents bought the car about a year before I got my license. For around $200, I think. It met a need—and little more. Despite its shortcomings, that car represented something much more significant to me: freedom. I was no different than just about any other teenager approaching his 16th birthday. From the time I started my driver's education, I had a plan to get my learner's permit, and then my driver's license, on the very first day I could possibly get them. My excitement for that rite of passage started even earlier, so that by the time I was finally old enough to get my license, the anticipation had been building for years.

Finally, the day came. I was a bundle of nerves as my road test began. I had heard the test would include some kind of attempt to trick me. That never happened. But there were a couple of moments when I questioned what the evaluator was asking me to do, followed by a silent look of contempt, and an ominous scratch on the paper with his pen. It wasn't helpful for my anxiety. Then came the worst part of the test: parallel parking. That task is hard enough as it is, let alone trying to nail it on the first try when anxiety is at its peak. Looking back all these years later, that part of the test is a blur in my memory. What I do remember is getting out of the car not knowing if I'd passed or failed. The silence was torture as the evaluator quietly finished his paperwork. *Scritch, scratch, scritch* . . . and then a swift tear along the perforated line as he handed me the copy I needed to get my license. It was a proud moment indeed. I walked back into that BMV office triumphantly, got my mug shot, and a few minutes later walked out with my license. I was beaming.

We got home and, not surprisingly, I was eager to experience my new freedom. I was going to drive somewhere . . . *anywhere*! I grabbed my wallet, a few bucks, and my boom box and took off for Taco Bell. Yep, my first trip as a new driver was a "run for the border." Burritos were calling, and now I had the freedom to go get them. *It. Was.*

Awesome! I remember that drive vividly. I remember how surreal it was to be alone in the car. I remember feeling a little like I was getting away with something. But most of all I remember feeling joy and a little bit of pride. Because, in addition to the freedom, I also felt like I had just taken a big step toward adulthood. Looking back, I think deep down, that was what I wanted the most: proof that I was growing up.

You probably have your own story with getting your license. It is a significant part of growing up in our Western culture. And it's not the only one. Rites of passage are deeply woven into our experiences. There are smaller ones like birthday parties, starting school, sleepovers, and summer camps. Then there are bigger ones like getting a license, starting your first job, high school graduation, moving away from home, joining the military, starting college, graduating from college, first dates, engagement, marriage . . . These are all things that mark important milestones in our lives. Make no mistake, they are important. But they are not, and never can be, what I think most of us always hoped they would be: an answer to our heart's deepest desires for validation.

In the last chapter we discussed the reality of generational momentum as a threat to the design of fatherhood. Fatherhood has indeed been a broken institution from the beginning. We have all been swept along in perpetual brokenness and, for the most part, largely unaware of it. Waking up to that reality is a necessary first step in recovering the promise of fatherhood for you and your family. In this chapter we are going to build on our awareness by taking a fresh look at a practice that has been prevalent through most of human history but almost entirely absent in our modern Western world: the ancient wisdom of initiation.

Cultures through human history have practiced initiation traditions for the express purpose of preparing boys (primarily) for the responsibilities of, and affirming their readiness for, adulthood. Many Native American traditions continue to practice some form of Vision

Quest as an initiation tradition. Tribal cultures around the world have initiation traditions involving bullet ants, whipping, cattle collecting, and feats of endurance to name a few. The Jewish tradition is for both boys and girls as they affirm a child's coming of age in Bar Mitzvah and Bat Mitzvah. And in Medieval Europe, the path to knighthood was a longstanding initiation tradition. In our family, initiation takes the form of a series of intimate ceremonies to affirm and celebrate each of our kids at key milestones in their lives. This is something I will explain a bit more throughout the book and in more detail in Appendix A.

I know how difficult many of these traditions are for a modern day Westerner to understand. What makes the topic even more confusing are some very negative associations with initiation used by gangs, fraternities, and secret societies that involve humiliation, self-mutilation, criminal behavior, and even murder. All of this can make it hard for some to embrace the idea in the first place. So we have some work to do.

One of my favorite verses in Scripture is from the New American Standard translation of Jeremiah 15:19:

> *. . . if you extract the precious from the worthless,*
> *you will become my spokesman.*

Through the years I have often come back to this invitation in God's words to the Israelites, words inviting them to view things for what is right and good. While a survey of initiation traditions around the world can be confusing, this is a topic that, with a little extraction, can lead us to something very precious indeed.

Let's start with the first point of confusion: the difference between rites of passage and initiation. Let me be direct: rites of passage and initiation are *not* the same thing. For those of us who have grown up in modern Western culture, that is a point we must be clear about. Because, unfortunately, somewhere along the line, we settled for rites of passage as a worthwhile substitute for the intentional practice of initiation and, in the process, lost something precious—and necessary: *the bestowing of sacred identity to our children.*

At a glance, the two concepts seem to be one and the same thing. But there is a key distinction that may seem small but, in reality, is essential in understanding our sacred role as fathers. What is that distinction? Simply put, it is two things: fierce intention and validation. We'll unpack both of these but, for now, know that intentionality and validation are not only the key differences between rites of passage and initiation, they are also key in understanding our sacred role as fathers.

Back to my story of getting that driver's license many years ago. What I was most aware of in the moment was the freedom that license could afford me. But there was something else I believed was happening. Even more important to me was what it meant in crossing a threshold toward adulthood. Deep down, I had come to believe that the achievement of obtaining my driver's license also validated the dawn of my adulthood. I was in search of validation for having crossed into a new status: my license was proof I had what it took to be a man. I suppose, for a while, it felt like it did just that. But over time it proved to be hollow. The evidence? I continued to look for the same sense of validation with each new rite of passage. Girlfriend? Hollow. High school graduation? Hollow. Moving away from home and starting college? Hollow. Buying my first new car? Hollow. Marriage, college graduation, military service, buying our first home, becoming a father, graduating seminary? All felt like things that could settle that question in my heart. *But they couldn't.* They were rites of passage, all good things worthy of celebrating and enjoying. However, what became more and more clear to me as the years went on was that I was searching for something in those milestone moments that was not—and never would be—there: validation.

From the beginning, a question was divinely placed in my heart, and yours, and it is meant to extract what is precious about the ancient wisdom of initiation. We must know what that question is. The question may take slightly different forms depending on life stages, personality, and circumstances, but each and every person is driven by extremely deep questions of identity. We are all desperately needing to know that we are worthy and loved. "Do I have what it takes?" "Am I valued/delighted in/respected/cherished?" These are core questions built deeply into the heart of every man, woman, and child. Those core questions cannot be answered for us by the mere passage of time or achievement, no matter how great or impressive the achievement is. Those divinely placed questions are born of our God-given desire to know who we are, what defines us, and what makes us worthy. The answers we hope to find to these questions are what drive our search for validation.

So we search, most of us believing, as Henri Nouwen put it, that we are what we do, what we have, or what others say we are.[2] The milestones celebrated in a rite of passage all seem to have the promise of answering our core questions because, on some level, they are a celebration of those three things. But what if our question cannot be answered by what we do, what we have, or what others say we are? We may feel, for a short time, that our questions are answered by title, possessions, or praise. But an honest examination reveals the truth: our questions don't go away. Which leaves most of us looking to the next rite of passage for our hope only to find that, sooner or later, the promise of finding peace for our hearts in these rites proves hollow. What starts as hope eventually gives way to disillusionment. Some respond by giving up and withdrawing; they are alive but hardly living. Others search ever more earnestly and eagerly to pursue their own rites of passage: ever more exotic adventures, more impressive endeavors, bigger achievements, better careers, or more income. Some turn to darker pursuits for answers (or even escape): sex, drugs, and alcohol, to name just a few.

It's not that rites of passage, themselves, are bad. They can be an important part of growing up. Most of these milestone moments are absolutely worth pursuing and celebrating, but they are not what we believed them to be. The issue at hand is not judgment on the worthiness of any particular rite of passage but the belief so many of us carry about what those milestones (or attempts to escape) can mean. And this brings us back to those divinely given core questions. These questions point us to something we were made to want and need. Our search for value, love, appreciation, and acceptance are all issues of identity, and the person who most of us instinctively look to first for our answer is our earthly father.

Men, your sacred role, your divine responsibility, lies in understanding this: fathers bestow identity to their kids. If you doubt this, I invite you to pause and reflect on your own story. As a little boy, what was your perception of your dad? If you're at all like me, he was a giant: strong and capable of anything! It's not a stretch to say he was a superhero to me. I went to my mom for comfort, encouragement, care, and nurture. In her arms I knew I was safe, protected, comforted, and encouraged. I looked to my dad for something else: I craved *approval, acceptance,* and *affirmation.* I craved his *attention* and *delight.* I loved it when he wrestled with me, played catch with me, put me in the child seat of his bike and rode with me. My heart needed his undivided love and attention because, within that, he was telling me I mattered, I was worthy, he believed in me. Even as a young boy, my core questions cried out for answers, and the first person I looked to for my answer was my dad. You likely did as well. Even if you grew up without a father, the desire was still there. And whether your memories are good, bad, or, as is the case for most, a mix, our dads gave us our first and probably most lasting answers to our questions. The emotions that stir within you as you look back and

> Men, your sacred role, your divine responsibility, lies in understanding this: fathers bestow identity to their kids.

reflect on your relationship with your own kids reveal this essential truth: fathers bestow identity to their kids.

Deep down, I think we've always known this. But instinctively knowing it and having unmistakable clarity around it are two different things. The lack of intentionality around bestowing identity and validation to our kids is one of the tragic casualties of losing touch with the ancient wisdom of initiation. We were most certainly made to want and need an earthly father who could guide us, teach us, train us, protect us, model for us, and, ultimately—in intimate partnership with our heavenly Father—bestow on us a deeply secure sense of identity. One who could "train us in the secrets" of finding answers to our core questions of identity and prepare us to live confidently in a world with infinite counterfeits. This is what all of us needed from our fathers. And it's what none of us truly got, certainly not to the full extent and with the fierce intentionality we truly needed. What we did have was an inadequate substitute. Rites of passage have failed to satisfy our questions, but where that fails, initiation can give us a framework to capture all of that promise. Where rites of passage lack intentionality, initiation cannot happen without it. Where rites of passage fail to answer our core questions, initiation is the result of a father's fierce intentionality to bestow identity to his kids.

How can we offer that to our kids if we have never known that initiation for ourselves? It is a riddle, isn't it?

If you're like me, though, this raises a bit of a question. How can we offer that to our kids if we have never known that initiation for ourselves? It is a riddle, isn't it? There is extremely good news, as it turns out. God is really good at it. You didn't get the initiation you wanted and needed from your father. God invites us all to see that clearly, grieve it with him, and be healed. This is where things get exciting. That healing includes learning to receive from him . . . to let our heavenly Father be for us what our earthly fathers were not or could not be. If we are going to stand against the current of generational momentum, somehow that riddle has to be solved. And it can be! So before you explore what it might look like to offer initiation to your kids, there is something here for you—an invitation you may not have seen coming.

It is an invitation for your own initiation.

MOUNTAIN CLIMBING

If people can't see what God is doing, they stumble all over themselves; But when they attend to what he reveals, they are most blessed (Proverbs 29:18, The Message).

I find so much hope in this proverb. It isn't stated directly, but the implication can't be missed. That I can see what God is doing and, in seeing it, realize the joy and blessing of living into what I now understand. This is your invitation to see and understand what God is doing in fathering you. And in seeing and understanding what he is doing, to live into something you may have never imagined: initiation into deeply intimate sonship with God. What does that look like? Let me start by sharing my initiation story.

In the first chapter I alluded to a major shake-up in my life that had me at a significant crossroads. To that point I had lived my entire life as a "mountain climber." Here's what that means: I believed the answer to my deep questions of identity could be found, primarily, in what I did and what others said about me. So achievement became essential as my primary way of garnering the praise and accolades my heart was so desperate for. I was aware of my desire to prove (to myself and the world around me) that I was valuable, that I mattered, and that I was worth celebrating, respecting, and accepting. In other words, I was on a mission to validate my worthiness to the world. However, I was totally unaware of the core questions about my identity that were behind my drive to achieve. I was compelled by an unnamed fear to perpetually search for achievement "mountains" that would keep the haunting taunts of shame and doubts about my worthiness at bay.

For about thirty-five years, this mountain climbing worked quite well for me. I simply kept repeating the formula: find a "mountain" to climb, climb it, receive the praise, respect, and awe I was looking for, and then do it all over again. As long as that kept working, I really had no reason to question it. So I kept climbing and achieving. I was a good student. I worked hard to excel athletically. I took great pride in having a reputation of being responsible and trustworthy. I graduated high school near the top of my class, graduated college with a degree in chemical engineering, and was commissioned as an officer in the Army. I worked for Ford Motor Company. We bought our first home. I married young and became a father. I was active in our church. One mountain led to the next.

Then came my biggest mountain yet: full-time vocational ministry. I set out on this next journey expecting the same cycle to repeat as it always had before. But this time things would be very different. Years of dysfunction were about to catch up to me. I had embarked on a journey that would shake me to my core and break me in the deepest places of my being.

It was the best thing that ever happened to me.

CRASH AND BURN

So I left my engineering job to go back to school and pursue a Master's degree in Theology. I graduated seminary and immediately poured myself into working alongside our long-time pastor to start a new church in Michigan. At first our experience was everything I'd hoped it would be. But, in truth, the same old pattern was repeating itself. I had many new opportunities to excel. And with that success came the praise and affirmation I had come to rely on. But as the demands of ministry grew, something was happening that I did not expect. I began to bump up against my limitations. I was getting tired. I found myself in the middle of broken lives, an arena I simply wasn't prepared for. Heck, I still hadn't recognized my own need for healing, let alone trying to minister to the needs of others. The growing demands of leading a small group, occasional preaching, video and audio editing, relationship building, leading set-up and tear-down teams for Sunday services, helping with kids ministry, meetings with other area pastors . . . all these were things that came with the job. But they were also creating demands that slowly but surely pushed me to the boundaries of my limitations.

I was finding it harder and harder to perform, and this meant that the sense of validation I had come to depend on was slowly vanishing as well. Things began to snowball as years of dysfunction finally brought me to my breaking point. I was failing, and the shame and fear I had always been able to keep at bay had finally caught me. I still didn't fully understand what was truly going on. All I knew was that things had become toxic for me, and the time had come for me to get away from it all.

It was a painful and difficult process for my wife and I to leave a church we had helped start. Ashamed, I wanted to run and hide. I hated going out of the house for fear I would see somebody I knew—something very hard to avoid in a small town. I was undone by the contempt I imagined everyone must have had for me. I set out on the journey with such hope and promise. Instead, I found myself in a dark new reality and, honestly, it felt like a death sentence. My entire life construct, built around a constant pursuit of validation in what I did and in what others said about me, had completely crumbled. It was my crash and burn. I was in uncharted territory. And I was afraid.

THE WILDERNESS

Desperate to escape this unfamiliar and uncomfortable wilderness, I tried to respond the way I always responded. Immediately, I went in search of another mountain. I gave serious consideration to going back to school so I could launch yet another career path. But something was different this time. There was something stirring in me that felt like a very serious warning. Not sure what to make of it, I assumed it was perhaps because I wasn't looking at the right mountain. So I asked some friends to help me. And that is when my world was rocked by my friend's suggestion that the time had come for me to simply be a dad.

I observed myself recoiling at the suggestion—and then felt the shame of having recoiled. What had happened that I found that idea so unworthy? I didn't like the disconnect that was now so abundantly clear and, in seeing that, I could now also begin to see clearly the warning I had only a sense of before. I was no longer able to ignore the man I had become. The warning had grown into a loud and clear command to stop. So, against every instinct, I did just that. I stopped.

It was maybe the hardest thing I ever did. Everything in me wanted to run. It felt like God was pouring judgment on me. Everything I had assumed that

> That is when my world was rocked by my friend's suggestion that the time had come for me to simply be a dad.

made me worthy of standing before him was gone. I felt utterly reject-ed and alone. There were no mountains. Only wilderness. Vast, vast expanses of wilderness. All I felt was shame. So, in the early going, I perceived my new reality as punishment. What I now know, though, is that it was a rescue. What I didn't know at the dawn of my days in the wilderness was that it wasn't the end of things . . . it was the beginning.

MY INITIATION

Those piercing words from my friend changed everything. Up to that moment, I had believed that my wilderness experience would be short-lived. In a flash, I now realized that God was not leading me out of the wilderness, he was leading me further in. So Mary Jo and I made the fateful decision that, instead of finding my way back into the workplace, I would stay home full-time with my kids while she worked full-time. My undoing continued. And my initiation began.

There were days it felt as though nothing was happening. There were long and dark stretches of isolation and silence—deafening si-lence. Other days felt like a set-up for humiliation. Anonymity was hard enough for me, but even worse were those moments that called me out. For some context, the whole idea of men being full-time, stay-at-home dads is much more common and generally accepted today than, say, even fifteen years ago. So as I went through my days taking care of my young son and daughter, I found myself having to adjust to the awkward reality of this chapter of my life. Everywhere I went with them and everything I did in being a father of young children inevita-bly had me surrounded by other stay-at-home parents—of course, all of them moms. So I stood out. I was a curiosity. Which, no doubt, was part of the reason I was asked *the* question so often. It was to the point of being comical (though I hardly saw the humor in it at the time). You may have guessed the question that I feared, and seemed unable to avoid: "What do you do for a living?"

I was asked by countless moms who, I think, weren't expecting the answer I reluctantly gave: "I'm a full-time dad." At the time, each time, it felt like I was saying: "I failed miserably as a servant of God, so the only thing left for me to do was take care of the kids." Then, of course, I felt the shame of feeling so dismissive of the important role of caring for my kids. I really did hate that question. But something was happening that, at first, I wasn't able to see. I was being *fathered*. In confronting me with the question and the uneasiness I felt in having to answer, I was unlearning my old assumptions about needing to prove my worthiness. Every time I spoke the words "I'm a full-time dad," I was forced to take an active step in unlearning thirty-five years of searching for validation. I now know that God was healing my sense of identity. Slowly things began to change. Then, one day, I was asked and I gave my answer—and I found that something wasn't there: shame. I still vividly remember the moment I felt Abba's warm smile and heard, deep in my heart: "Well done, son. Welcome home."

It was a profound turning point for me that, even as I'm typing these words, stirs up deeply emotional joy of that moment. For the first time in my life I had begun to experience the freedom of feeling loved and worthy without anything of note that I could offer as a reason. No title, no past or future achievement . . . no "proof" of any kind that I had to offer. In the anonymity of full-time stay-at-home fatherhood, I was learning for the first time in my life what it felt like to no longer need any of those things to feel worthy. I was learning what had been true all along but I had never been able to receive: that I was Abba's beloved son and that was (and always had been) more than enough. That the very premise of needing to prove my worthiness never had been and never would be God's heart toward me. I was beginning to receive the validation I had always longed for and had spent so much of my life looking for in all the wrong places. God was initiating me into intimate sonship with him.

That is your invitation as well. Maybe you can relate to being a mountain climber, maybe you can't. Regardless, we have something in common. We have core questions of identity we have shaped our lives around in pursuit of answers. Whether you have pursued validation by trying to prove your worthiness or whether you have withdrawn, taken out by the haunting voices of shame that have felt like the final word of your worth, your journey to recovering your good father's heart starts with God's hopeful invitation. Your heavenly Father knows what you need, he knows what you never received, and he is inviting you to receive from him what your heart is crying out for: validation that does not require proof and cannot be earned. You are loved. You belong. You are his son, and you have nothing to prove. Your intentional Father is calling out to you. Your initiation awaits.

OKAY, BUT WHAT ABOUT MY KIDS?

I get it. You're a dad. You still carry your desire to be an intentional dad with your own kids. So you are eager to learn what that might look like. By now, though, I hope you see and understand your own need for healing and initiation. You can't give what you don't have.

Still, you're eager to see at least a little bit of a bigger picture. I understand your desire; I had the same burning questions. So let me share just a little bit more of my initiation story and give you what God gave me at this point of my journey.

In learning the lessons of my initiation, something else started to become clear: my responsibility to my children to teach them what I was now learning. I may have been reluctant and uneasy in my early days in the wilderness and in my new role as a stay-at-home dad, but I was also committed to recovering my father's heart. As God was fathering me to start receiving my validation from him, I was also beginning to see my responsibility to my kids to teach them to do the same. Even in those early days, one thing was extremely clear:

this wasn't going to happen by accident. Quite the opposite. This was going to require a very committed and intentional kind of fathering, the kind of intentionality I think Paul's words to the Philippians hint at:

> *I have been trained in the secret*
> *of overcoming all things*
> (4:12, 13, The Passion)

Yes, trained! Paul's story is an inspiring story of a man very intimately trained by God. He was a man who knew what it was to be fathered. And in being fathered as a beloved son walking intimately with Abba, he says he was trained. Trained in what? The secret of *overcoming all things.* Yes! This stirs my father's heart. Oh, how I want my kids to be able to say the same thing.

Abba was very intentional with Paul. He offers that same intentionality to you and me. And in our divine responsibility of fatherhood, we are invited to share in that intentionality with him on behalf of our kids. As my own heart as a father was being healed, I was also reawakening to my sacred role. I could now see my most important responsibility as a dad: bestow a deeply secure sense of identity in my kids as God's beloved sons/daughter. In my initiation, I had also awakened to God's invitation to walk intimately with him on a very intentional road to do just that.

I had much more to learn about God's design for fatherhood, things we will explore later in this book. For now, though, a pattern was established that, all these years later, has not and will not change. In being fathered, I was learning to father my children. It is a pattern we first learn for ourselves that we then offer to our kids: fierce intentionality around bestowing a deeply secure sense of identity and training that prepares them for this intimate life of daughtership, or sonship, with God.

Men, isn't that what your father's heart is moved by? That you could learn God's design for your life of intimate belovedness* with him and, in doing that, learn your sacred role as a father and be invited alongside him with fierce intentionality to train your kids, usher them through their childhood, and launch them into adulthood? To, as Brennan Manning wrote, "define themselves radically as one beloved by God" (*Abba's Child*, p. 51). That is initiation. It's what you needed and didn't get. The same does not need to be true for your kids.

If you are going to turn against the tide of generational momentum for you and your kids, you must first learn to receive from God what you did not receive from your dad. Again, you can't give what you don't have. Before rushing to the question of how to initiate your kids, you must first learn what it is to live as a beloved son—to be initiated into intimate sonship with Abba. Back to the key truth: you are loved. You belong. You are his son, and you have nothing to prove. Your Intentional Dad is calling out to you. Your initiation awaits.

Next: The life of belovedness with God is indeed your birthright. Awakening to that is the first step toward Abba's invitation for you.

*Okay, for any grammar stewards out there, I know that technically this is not a word. Even so, it is language I have used in my community and with my family for years. Made up or not, it communicates the foundational idea of our deepest and truest identity: the eternally secure state of being delighted in and beloved. So, going forward, you will see this word (okay, non-word) used often.

Chapter Four

THE MATRIX

This is your last chance. After this, there is no turning back. You take the blue pill, the story ends, you wake up in your bed, and believe whatever you want to believe. You take the red pill, you stay in Wonderland, and I show you how deep the rabbit hole goes. Remember, all I'm offering is the truth—nothing more.
—Morpheus, *The Matrix*[1]

One of the things that surprised me when I first read the New Testament seriously was that it talked so much about a Dark Power in the universe—a mighty, evil spirit who was held to be the Power behind death, disease, and sin . . . Christianity thinks this Dark Power was created by God, and was good when he was created, and went wrong. Christianity agrees . . . this is a universe at war.
—C. S. Lewis[2]

We had just pulled into the parking lot. We had some shopping to do, and this was the first stop of many we would make that day. As we got out of the car I immediately noticed a young man coming toward me.

His body language told me he was in need and in search of help. Sure enough, he began telling me about his broken down car a few blocks away. I really don't remember too many other details about his story, but what he was asking for and the need he described was enough, as best I could tell, to pass the smell test. He was just looking for a few dollars to help solve his problem. Yes, there was a part of me that wondered if he was trying to play me. It certainly wasn't the first time I found myself interacting with a stranger asking for money. And it's always a bit of a puzzle to try to discern what the truth might be in these stories, always a bit of a dilemma for me as I balance the plight of a fellow human being with the very real possibility that my desire to help will only enable something destructive. So, here again, I found myself trying to exercise some discernment. But I leaned toward helping him out. I gave him a few dollars, and we went our separate ways.

The very next day we were in a different shopping center not far from our stop the day before. This time, we were coming out of a store and, just as we were about to get into our car, I looked up and—you guessed it—that same young man was walking toward me. It was a re-play, word for word, of the day before. He started to tell the exact same story leading to the exact same request. He looked at me expectantly as I stared back at him with a mix of anger and sadness. The day before I gave him the benefit of the doubt. Now I knew I had misjudged and, unfortunately, played a part in enabling his dishonest life. Clearly, this man did not remember our encounter from the day before, because he was genuinely surprised and embarrassed as I explained to him how odd it was that just the day before he had come to me with the exact same story. I calmly told him how disappointing it was to realize that I had been scammed by a man I wanted to believe was being honest. His stunned silence said it all: exposed. I just looked at him as we got into our car. He said nothing and slowly walked away.

Have you ever felt like there is more going on than you can see? That there is more to the story than you're being told? That you're not quite seeing the whole picture or, worse, that the story you're being told isn't even close to what's really going on? You probably have your own story of being lied to and scammed. Mine is, in the end, quite minor. I lost a few bucks and got duped into enabling a man's dishonesty. Others, perhaps even you, have devastating stories of betrayal and loss. But even in my relatively insignificant experience here, we can see a fundamental element of scams that is common to all of them, big or small. What made it possible for the scam to unfold, what it was dependent on, was my acceptance of a false reality. In order to maintain that, a scammer must, at all costs, keep somebody from seeing things as they really are. Exposure is a death sentence for a lie of any kind.

Up to this point, I've only alluded to it. In awakening to your sacred role as a father, seeing the way generational momentum has silently been sweeping you along and thwarting your fatherhood journey, and hearing God's invitation for your own initiation into intimate sonship, we have taken some necessary steps to seeing a more complete picture of your divine responsibility as a father. We are beginning to see things as they really are—as though we've been shielded from seeing them before. Perhaps you've always had a sense that there is more going on than you can see, that you're not quite getting the whole picture. Or maybe you're just starting to awaken to that feeling. For many, though, some very direct words are needed: *there is so much more to the story of your day-to-day life than you can see.* I'm afraid another casualty of

> I'm afraid another casualty of growing up in a modern Western culture is the dismissal of anything supernatural. We come from a culture of the tangible, explainable, measurable, and (maybe most importantly) controllable.

growing up in a modern Western culture is the dismissal of anything supernatural. We come from a culture of the tangible, explainable, measurable, and (maybe most importantly) controllable. But what if the physical world simply isn't the whole picture of reality? And what if there are forces that are invested in keeping you blind to that, forces working quite deliberately to keep from being exposed? At this point in your journey, it will no longer do to hint at and allude to that possibility. The remainder of this book, I'm afraid, simply will not make sense unless we first come to understand this reality together. So, before we go further, the time has come to expose the forces that have lingered, unrecognized in the shadows, forces that have been working hard to keep you from seeing things as they truly are.

So here we are, much like that famous scene in *The Matrix* with Morpheus and Neo sitting across from one another. Neo is at a crossroads. He got to this point because of a nagging sense that what he experienced in his day-to-day life was mostly an illusion. In a series of white knuckle events he has finally come to this place, with Morpheus, on the cusp of having the illusion fully exposed. Morpheus affirms Neo's suspicions but, wisely, takes this moment to help Neo see as clearly as possible the choice before him. The wisdom of this is important enough that I ask you to look again at these words offered at the start of this chapter.

This is your last chance. After this, there is no turning back. You take the blue pill, the story ends, you wake up in your bed, and believe whatever you want to believe. You take the red pill, you stay in Wonderland, and I show you how deep the rabbit hole goes. Remember, all I'm offering is the truth—nothing more.

You too are now at a crossroads. In awakening to God's invitation for your own initiation, you should know what you are moving toward. Vague inklings and internal whispers simply won't do anymore. Your journey forward is toward God's invitation, but it is jealously guarded by forces heavily invested in keeping you blind to a bigger reality, to what is really going on. Like Neo, you are awakening to things as they really are; you are awakening to a reality that will change . . . everything. As you reach for the red pill, remember: all I'm offering is the truth—nothing more.

KNOW YOUR ENEMY

Let's start with the simple truth: you have an enemy who has hated you from the beginning and, driven by pride, malice, and contempt, has been working in opposition to you and God . . . every day of your life. Did you catch that? This enemy *hates* you! He hates your very existence. He hates the way you look, think, and act. He hates that you breathe, eat, and drink. And he hates most that you're loved, cherished, pursued—that you are the object of God's deepest affections. Why? Because, above all, he hates God. This enemy is known by many names: Lucifer, the serpent, the dragon, the opposer, the accuser, Beelzebub, the Devil, and Satan. Jesus has a few names for him too. He calls him a thief saying:

> *"The thief comes only to steal and kill and destroy . . ."*
> (John 10:10).

He also calls him a murderer and the father of lies:

> *"He was a murderer from the beginning, not holding to the truth, for there is no truth in him. When he lies, he speaks his native language, for he is a liar and the father of lies"* (John 8:44).

No doubt, this isn't the first time you've heard about this formidable enemy. But hearing about him and taking him seriously—very seriously—are two entirely different things. And the idea of taking him seriously is a new, and frankly unnerving, idea for many. If you are feeling a bit skeptical at this point, let me start by saying, I appreciate your misgivings. Like many of you, I have seen and heard some awfully strange things in the name of this spiritual reality. So I know your doubts because I too have had them. Here again, I think we have another invitation to extract the precious from the worthless. As C.S. Lewis wisely observed in his book *The Screwtape Letters*:

There are two equal and opposite errors into which our race can fall about the devils. One is to disbelieve in their existence. The other is to believe, and to feel an excessive and unhealthy interest in them. They themselves are equally pleased by both errors.[3]

So, taking Lewis's cue, let's start by discarding the two extremes that are worthless: giving Satan and his legion of fallen angels too much credit or, even worse, ignoring them altogether.

In the first, he is to blame for every sin and shortcoming in our lives. He becomes an easy way to circumvent responsibility for our own failures and brokenness. "The devil made me do it" is a saying that becomes an evil itself as it's used as license for all kinds of destruction, deceit, and abuse. It can also lead to a life of paranoia, a life shaped around fear of insurmountable spiritual threats around every corner. This extreme is not healthy or helpful.

The other extreme, ignoring him, in my experience is more common and maybe even more consequential. Lies require deception to survive. Schemers work extremely hard to keep their victims from seeing things

> The other extreme, ignoring him, in my experience is more common and maybe even more consequential. Lies require deception to survive.

as they are. What makes this extreme more consequential is that, in ignoring him, we are choosing to allow his work to continue unopposed. And what is his work? Stealing. Killing. Destroying. Accusing. Lying. Dividing. Diminishing. You see the fruits of his work every day. You had an argument with your wife. It never crosses your mind that there was an enemy at work fanning the flames of misunderstanding and accusation. Your son is having trouble with bullying tormentors at school. It never crosses your mind that there is an enemy orchestrating the hatred. You and your dad haven't spoken in years, and you shrug indifferently, chalking it up to two grown men who have simply grown apart. So the thief continues his schemes entirely unopposed, unchecked. You remain ignorant to his work in twisting, accusing, lying, orchestrating, and manipulating his way into the hearts and minds of humanity and his corruption of God's creation, blind to his impact on each and every one of us. All the while he goes on undermining you, your heart, your family, your fatherhood. He continues, unopposed, distorting your perception of God, yourself, and others, cleverly sowing seeds of distrust that turn us against each other. In other words, he has you right where he wants you. So while I understand and can relate to your skepticism, let me put it plainly. You can continue ignoring the reality of an enemy on the prowl in your life, but you cannot do that and pursue God's invitation for initiation into intimate sonship with him. You cannot have it both ways.

Why? Closing your eyes to something doesn't make it go away. If you have young children you may have been unaware of the moment your children started to learn this. If you've ever played peek-a-boo with a young child, you are actually participating in an essential element of their development called "object permanence." You've very likely played that game, hiding your face with your hands or a blanket and quickly revealing your face as you say "peek-a-boo." What they are learning is that seeing or not seeing an object is not related to whether it is really there. They are learning object permanence. For a baby, this concept actually takes a little while to make sense. As they get older, you can see the development of this concept in what they understand about the game of hide and seek. Some young kids will "hide" simply by closing their eyes—if I can't see you, you can't see me. They are still developing their sense of object permanence.

Which brings us back to the ultimate enemy. Closing your eyes to his presence and his work does not make him go away. You may be intrigued by, and drawn to, God's invitation for you and your family. But staying blind to the reality of an enemy opposed to that, I'm afraid, will only result in you stepping into that invitation unprepared, unaware, and easily picked off.

How, then, do we get to what is precious? How do we reject the worthless of the two extremes and draw out of this what we need to know? Let's go back to the beginning so that, as the old saying goes, we might "know our enemy."

The beginning would be Genesis, right? The serpent? Actually, no. The story of our enemy goes back further. As we'll see, his backstory comes before humanity enters the story. The prophet Ezekiel offers us a glimpse into this backstory through a lament from God directed at a mysterious "king of Tyre" (Ezekiel 28).

> *You were the seal of perfection, full of wisdom and perfect in beauty. You were in Eden, the garden of God . . . (vv. 12, 13).*

This mysterious "king," then, was quite the spectacle: perfect in beauty and full of wisdom.

> *You were anointed as a guardian cherub,*
> *for so I ordained you. You were on the holy mount*
> *of God; you walked among the fiery stones (v. 14).*

Furthermore, this "king" had a high office of honor, a place among God's inner circle, ordained as a guardian cherub.

You were blameless in your ways from
the day you were created (v. 15).

This is lofty language indeed. Whoever this "king" is, one thing is certain: this is no ordinary being. He was full of wisdom, perfect in beauty, had a place on the holy mount of God walking among the fiery stones (sounds quite exclusive!), was ordained as a guardian . . . and freely roamed Eden. There is no missing an aura of awe and splendor in this description. But something went very, very wrong.

. . . till wickedness was found in you. Through your widespread
trade you were filled with violence, and you sinned (vv. 15, 16).

Wickedness and violence enter the story. God was forced to act.

So I drove you in disgrace from the mount of God, and I expelled
you, guardian cherub, from among the fiery stones (v. 16).

What a fall! Grace and splendor ended in a humiliating rebuke. The judgment is severe.

Your heart became proud on account of your beauty,
and you corrupted your wisdom because of your splendor. So I
threw you to the earth; I made a spectacle of you before kings
(v. 17, emphasis mine).

What started as a beautiful, powerful, glorious being loved and honored by God became corrupted by pride. Something happened, and God responded with swift and decisive judgment. What happened? Open rebellion.

Then war broke out in heaven. Michael and his angels fought
against the dragon, and the dragon and his angels fought back.
But he was not strong enough, and they lost their place in heaven.
The great dragon was hurled down—that ancient serpent called the
devil, or Satan, who leads the whole world astray. He was
hurled <u>to the earth, and his angels with him</u>
(Revelation 12:7-9, emphasis mine).

War? Rebellion? A fierce battle between Michael and those who re-mained loyal to God versus Satan and those who joined him in rebel-lion? This is not a tame and polite story. Pride corrupted the wisdom, splendor, and beauty of this "king of Tyre." His pride led to a jealous rebellion to seize God's glory for himself. He gambled and lost it all. His fate? Expulsion from the inner circle of the mount of God. He was hurled out. Where? *Earth!* Did you catch that? And did you notice, it wasn't just the leader of this rebellion? So, too, all the angels who joined in the rebellion were hurled to earth with him!

What a battle that must have been. The clash of the full might of good and evil had to be a terrible spectacle. The battle came to a cli-max, and Michael and his heavenly host secured victory. But notice: the enemy and his legion of rebels was not destroyed. They lived on. They may have suffered a defeat, a humiliating one. But we all know that, until the enemy is completely eliminated, the story isn't truly over. This ultimate enemy of God didn't wilt away in shame and hu-mility never to be heard from again. His plan for open war against God had failed. So he licked his wounds and pursued a new strategy, with his legion of fallen angels, to wage his war. This time, his target would be *you.*

This changes everything. Whether you realize it or not, you have been living your life in a story. Perhaps your story has been life as a pursuit of comfort and happiness. Or maybe, as is my story, your story has been one of attaining praise, respect, and honor. Perhaps you have come to see the primary backdrop of your story as duty, politics, or maybe security or achievement. But the reality is that most of us have lived in very small stories blind to the real context of our lives. We have been lured into accepting a false reality and have paid dearly for it. Waking up to things as they really are, the true story in which we live, is absolutely necessary if we are going to follow God into intimate sonship and intentional fatherhood. Please go back and look at the C.S. Lewis quote at the top of this chapter. Lewis's point: the reality we all live in is a universe at war.

This reality is the backdrop across every page of Scripture. Moses, Ezekiel, Isaiah, David, Solomon, the Psalms, Proverbs, Job, Peter, Paul, John, and Jesus himself tell us again and again that our reality, the context for your life and mine, is war! This is your reality whether you see it or not. And even more sobering is the realization that the objective in this war, the prize at the center of this epic conflict between good and evil, is you and your heart. The enemy, and his dark angels with him, have their hatred, malice, and contempt squarely sighted on you, your family, and every person you have ever cared about. So it simply will not do to ignore this reality any longer. Nor will it do to respond in despair or helpless irresponsibility. Far from either extreme, you have a place in this story. Your enemy greatly fears you finding your place and discovering your strength and capacity for opposing him.

Now that you are reoriented to this reality, we're ready to go deeper into the rabbit hole. There is more of the Matrix we need to expose for you to find your way in this new reality. Let's continue our awakening to things as they really are—exposing exactly what our enemy is after and his methods for getting it.

THE ANATOMY OF HIS SCHEME

How, then, can you begin to find your place in this epic story of war? Well, just as exposure undermined the scheme of the young man I encountered on our shopping trips, so the schemes of our enemy will begin to crumble with exposure. Sure, our enemy is more sophisticated in his schemes than the young man I came across those two days. But underneath the sophisticated maneuvering and clever efforts to keep us occupied with a false reality is a surprisingly simple playbook. And once you start to recognize "the plays," those schemes are no different from any other. They fall apart from exposure. Jesus said it himself: Satan, the serpent, is the father of lies working hard to keep you invested in a false reality. So the key to exposing the lies is to get good at looking beyond what is said to see what he's trying accomplish with those lies. What emerges is shockingly simple. Let's go back to that fateful moment when this fallen cherub takes his rebellion to his new target: humanity. The sad and devastating story picks up in Genesis chapter 3.

> *The serpent was clever, more clever than any wild animal God had made. He spoke to the Woman: "Do I understand that God told you not to eat from any tree in the garden?"*
>
> *The Woman said to the serpent, "Not at all. We can eat from the trees in the garden. It's only about the tree in the middle of the garden that God said, 'Don't eat from it; don't even touch it or you'll die.'"*
>
> *The serpent told the Woman, "You won't die. God knows that the moment you eat from that tree, you'll see what's really going on. You'll be just like God, knowing everything, ranging all the way from good to evil."*
>
> *When the Woman saw that the tree looked like good eating and realized what she would get out of it—<u>she'd know everything!</u>—she took and ate the fruit and then gave some to her husband, and he ate*
> (Genesis 3:1-6, The Message, emphasis added).

I don't know that there is a more tragic story in all of Scripture. It all seems so promising in the beginning. God is on the scene, and he has a project—a big one. God is creating the heavens and the earth. He starts with "nothingness" and "emptiness." He speaks into existence the raw materials he will use to create. Bit by bit he brings order and beauty out of the chaos. Light and Dark, Sea and Sky, Land, Plants, Day governed by the sun, Night governed by the moon, the construct of time, animal life on the land and in the sea and, finally, humans. And oh, how proud he was of humans! With each milestone of creation God looked upon his work and called it good—which, coming from God, is no small thing. But when he finished creating humanity, he looked upon his work and called it *very* good! David is one of many to observe this deep affinity God has for humanity:

What is mankind that you are mindful of them, human beings that you care for them? You have made them a little lower than the angels and crowned them with glory and honor (Psalm 8:4, 5).

A little lower than angels! Crowned with glory and honor! It is all so . . . good. So very good. The story continues, and a beautiful picture of intimacy, belonging, and purpose emerges. God's creation was an outpouring of love, a gift from him for humanity. But it all takes a very jarring, dark turn. I can almost hear the ominous background music as the serpent enters the scene. We're told he's clever—very clever. He's on the prowl.

We now know the backstory of this dark serpent. We know what he risked, what he lost, and the wicked pride that fueled his rebellion. He has been judged, rebuked, and rejected . . . but not eliminated. We also know that his judgment included being thrown to the earth, along with all fallen angels who joined him in that rebellion. At this point of the story, earth is untainted. God's creation is uncorrupted by evil. In his exile, the enemy is cast to earth, but, as we learn, that exile on earth does not include an exile from Eden. By the way: I am aware of the questions all of this raises about God and evil. These are issues of great theological debate that could fill an entire book. That, of course, is not the point of this book. So, putting those questions aside, let's simply come back to what is important here for us: we have an enemy, his rebellion continues, and the target of his war is the human heart.

So this cunning enemy slithers onto the scene, and he's on the prowl looking for an opportunity to continue waging his war. Only this time, he has a new strategy and a new target. Since he cannot go directly after the God he hates, he turns his malice toward what God loves most. So the stage is set and the predator has singled out his prey: the woman—innocent and unsuspecting, it would seem. He wastes no time in setting her up. A lie. Right off the bat. It would seem he intends for Eve to see through this one, though, because her quick rebuttal didn't phase him. Instead, it seemed to fuel him. This first lie drew her in. She knows what God has told them about the Tree of Knowledge of Good and Evil, so she sets the record straight about what God said, that he only warned of death about the tree in the middle of the garden. But the serpent is clever—extremely clever. Swiftly, he seizes on his prey by setting his true trap. A lie so compelling it puts Eve on the cusp of throwing it all away. A lie so compelling it has Adam paralyzed in inaction. (Notice in verse 6 that he was right there all along, an observation explored in detail by Dr. Larry Crabb, Al Andrews, and Don Hudson in *The Silence of Adam*.) And what makes this lie so compelling? Don't just look at the words he uses, look at what the serpent is targeting with those words.

"You won't die!"

It is unspoken, but still very much communicated. With this one lie, the enemy plants a seed of doubt about God's goodness and trust-worthiness. What wasn't explicitly said, but quite intentionally communicated, is this: "This God you think you can love and trust, this God who has placed limitations on you, what makes you so sure he is worthy of your trust? What makes you so sure he is good? What if he's a liar? He says you will die, but have you considered his real reasons for telling you that?" An unsuspecting Eve and a dumbfounded Adam, now ensnared for the first time by doubts about God's goodness and trustworthiness, are set up. They are blind to what the serpent is really doing. So the serpent moves in for the kill.

"God knows that the moment you eat from that tree, you'll see what's really going on. You'll be just like God, knowing everything, ranging all the way from good to evil."

Again, don't just look at what is said, see beyond the words to what is implied by this devious creature: "Isn't it obvious? The real reason he told you not to eat from that tree is that he fears you figuring out that you can be just like him! So it makes sense that he would tell you something to scare you away. The thing he doesn't want you to know is that *you can be more . . . so much more*. You can be his equal!" And with that, the war had now come to an unsuspecting Adam and Eve. They are now on the cusp of destroying everything. It all happens so fast, and it all seemed so frighteningly easy for the enemy to accomplish. What, exactly, did he do? What was it that Adam and Eve both seemed so unprepared to resist? When you take a moment to peel it all back, to boil it down, the devastating effect of his lies that, in a flash, had Adam and Eve considering the unthinkable, wasn't in what was explicitly said, it was in what was very much *communicated*. And what was communicated was two deadly, intertwined ideas:

1) God isn't good.

2) You're not good enough.

As we discussed in the last chapter, every man, woman, and child carries with them extremely deep questions about their value and worthiness of love. These core questions are questions of identity. The human story, yours and mine, is one of a desperate search for answers and validation for those core questions. Your story and mine is, as Henri Nouwen says in *Spiritual Direction*, one of a search for answers in what we do, what we have, or what others say about us.[4] But why are we so desperately searching? Because we are all carrying the burden of doubt and a fear that we aren't worthy of love. And since our core questions don't go away, we desperately run after anything that seems to carry the promise to answer our questions and put our fears to rest. But take a close look at that doubt. When you boil it down, at the center of our unresolved core questions about identity, are two deadly, intertwined ideas. You guessed it:

1) God isn't good.

2) You're not good enough.

To this point, you have been blind to his schemes. But his playbook is shockingly simple. He is a liar and schemer. He is clever. Behind all of his sophisticated schemes, though, we see his two intertwined weapons of war. And he has been playing all of humanity since. That includes you, your wife, your children, your coworkers, your neighbors, your friends, your family. It includes me and my family—even as I write this chapter. Here is a snapshot into how things have gone for us just in the last week.

A few days ago, I woke early. There was no particular reason. I lay in bed a bit longer thinking I might fall back asleep. But I couldn't. Something had started to churn inside me, and my heart was heavy. I sensed an invitation from God to get up and walk with him around the neighborhood before the family got up. I started my walk, hopeful that the invitation I sensed would bring some relief from this cloud. I tried some prayer but felt . . . distant. I tried taking a moment to appreciate the beauty of some flowers but felt . . . indifferent. I tried listening to birds but felt . . . boredom. Hardly what I was hoping for. So I paused to see if I could put words to the heaviness I was feeling. Discouragement. Inadequacy. Diminishment. I felt a general atmosphere of ridicule, mockery, and accusation about nearly every facet of my life: fatherhood, ministry, writing this book, and caring for my wife, family, friends, and neighbors. And in the midst of that cloud, it was easy to imagine a distant God looking on me with impatience, condemnation, and maybe even disgust.

But I'd seen and heard this before. This was a scheme. One I have come to recognize because of what was behind each and every feeling and thought I was wrestling with. It wasn't explicit, but it was very much communicated. You guessed it.

1) God isn't good.

2) I'm not good enough.

And it wasn't just me. My family gave me permission to share glimpses into their weeks as well. My wife shared with me a growing awareness of some feelings of sometimes not being enough. My oldest son has been sorting through similar struggles. My daughter has been experiencing the negative impact of a fear of failure. My youngest son has expressed frustration with feeling overlooked at times. And what do all of these struggles have in common? Yep, there they are again— the unspoken but still very much communicated intertwined ideas:

1) God isn't good.

2) You're not good enough.

Here's what I've come to know: this isn't just a theme I battle in my own life. It isn't just a theme with my family. The ancient story of the serpent targeting Adam and Eve is actually a massive exposure of the scheme the serpent has been working on against each and every one of us from that day to this. Sit with that revelation for a minute. As you reflect on your own story. As you think about the pain that surfaces in exploring your story, the core questions of identity and the search for answers that have shaped your life. How much of that story can be understood through the impact of these two intertwined lies? Why is it that we are so desperate to find validation? What is it that drives us on this never-ending search for value, love, and worth in what we have, what we do, or what others say about us?

Until the serpent came along, Adam and Eve knew nothing of doubts about God's goodness, and they certainly had never questioned their value and worthiness of love. They were completely secure, perfectly rooted in their sacred identities. That sacred identity is exactly what the serpent targeted and continues to target with each and every one of us. With deadly precision, he unleashes his scheme to rob us of our birthright. We have all fallen prey to his schemes, and what you and I have forfeited because of the deceit is no less devastating than what Adam and Eve forfeited. They bought into the lies, and we have all taken our turn in doing the same. We have all been trying to claw our way back to Eden ever since. The enemy keeps running the same scheme, and he has humanity collectively chasing its tail.

> They bought into the lies, and we have all taken our turn in doing the same. We have all been trying to claw our way back to Eden ever since.

We have been blind to what the "thief" is truly after. No, it's worse. We have ignored and even rejected the idea of his very presence. Much has been lost. The effect has been devastating—and not in a distant, "general" sense. Your story, my story, each and every human being, has been stung by the grief, loss, suffering, pain, and devastation born of the schemes of the enemy to sow seeds of doubt about the goodness of God and our sacred identities as his beloved sons and daughters. The time has come to awaken, beloved son. And now that you are ready to take him seriously, now that you are seeing things as they really are, the schemes are already beginning to lose their power. He is being exposed, and you are already becoming a far more formidable threat. James teaches:

<u>Resist</u> the devil and he will flee from you (4:7, emphasis added).

As my morning walk earlier this week continued, I awakened to what was really going on—and something happened. It took me a while to recognize it but, eventually, I realized that the serpent had been cleverly working his scheme again. I needed a moment to assess the heaviness I was feeling and look at what was behind it. The false reality of a God impatient and disgusted with my inadequacies and so-called "failures" fell away. I saw what was really happening and the sudden silence of those nagging thoughts said it all. Exposed. The weight I had been feeling and the cloud that had been hanging over me lifted. And far from an impatient and disappointed God, I found myself received by an encouraging embrace from my heavenly Father—and a warm invitation to talk with him about my wife, my children, my ministry, and my book. I withstood the scheme. I pushed back. I resisted.

No, it isn't always that easy. In fact, often it takes much more of a fight. The point is, though, as James said, I resisted and he fled. You can do the same. It will no longer do to ignore and pretend, to continue living in a small story far removed from the reality of a universe at war. The Matrix is being exposed for the illusion that it is. You are beginning to understand your enemy, to "know him." And with what you know, already you have become a far more formidable threat to him and his schemes. But there is more to this war than a good defense. Yes: resist. Withstand. Push back. He will flee.

But that is only the beginning. Your divine responsibility to bestow sacred identity to your children starts with a recovery of your sacred identity. God is inviting you to take your place in the story to get it back: first for yourself, then for your kids and family. By now I suspect it's become clear to you: you're going to have to fight for it. Let's get ready for battle.

Next: The enemy has something that belongs to you. You have been the victim of his schemes and have been duped into forfeiting your birthright. What's needed is a recovery of your sacred identity.

Chapter Five

AND SO IT BEGINS

"For this people's heart has become calloused; they hardly hear with their ears, and they have closed their eyes. Otherwise they might see with their eyes, hear with their ears, understand with their hearts and turn, <u>and I would heal them</u>" (Matthew 13:15, emphasis added).

But you, God, see the trouble of the afflicted; you consider their grief and take it in hand. The victims commit themselves to you; you are the helper of the fatherless (Psalms 10:14).

"A wound that goes unacknowledged and unwept is a wound that cannot heal."
—John Eldredge[1]

How will I feed my babies?"

It wasn't just the words she said, it was the way she said them. The fear in my mom's voice was unsettling to say the least. I very much remember the silence that hung in the air as she looked at my dad . . . who had nothing to say. He just looked back at her and, after a few tense moments, my Mom stormed upstairs, slammed the bedroom door, and cried. I think I was about nine years old. Money, or the lack of it, always seemed to be a cloud of tension in my family. And on this day, my Mom had, once again, reached a breaking point.

My dad had a difficult time consistently providing for our family.* This wasn't the first time the tension had spilled over. I was very familiar with heated discussions about what to pay, who to pay, who not to pay, how to pay it, and when. There were arguments about how long we could put off paying the electricity or phone bills before they got shut off, and this wasn't the first time my mom worried aloud about how we were going to pay for groceries. Of course, I couldn't help but feel the tension as well and have my own worries about electricity or having enough food to eat. But this time there was a big difference as I watched this familiar argument play out. This time I had another option besides absorbing it all with helpless anxiety.

It just so happened that I had recently started my very first job. I actually had a job as a nine-year-old. Once a week I delivered a local newspaper. It was my job to get the stacks of papers, stuff them with ads, roll and rubber band them, fill our wagon, and deliver them to our neighborhood homes. It was a big route, and it took most of my day. So I worked hard and, as you can imagine, felt great pride when I got that first paycheck.

So there I was, looking at my dad still standing there and listening to my mom crying upstairs. My family was in need and, this time, I knew I could help. So I went up to my room, got my check, and came back down and offered it to my dad. My dad took the check. I didn't know it then, but that would prove to be a wound that would silently shape my life for the next twenty-seven years.

*All of this is shared with my Dad's permission. In fact it's much more than that. If you'd like, read more in acknowledgements. My mother has since passed away.

My dad offered many wonderful things to me as a kid. Most significant were his time and presence. I can't remember any significant event of my childhood when he wasn't there. Activities, sports, school events—it was rare for him to not be there. Which makes this such a hard chapter to write. Earlier in the book I only touched on the truth that my dad had wounded me—the same as your dad with you. So I hate that my dad will be one of many men reading this. I don't like how this may hurt him. And I truly do not enjoy saying it. But I learned long ago just how essential it was for me to go into my story even if it meant I would have to face some really difficult and uncomfortable things. I had reached a point in my life that I could see, with alarming clarity, just how much my heart was in need of serious care. I was undone at the realization that my brokenness was already having an impact on my children and, unless something changed, I was only going to continue a legacy of unredeemed wounding from father to son and father to daughter. That meant there was only one way forward: diving deep into my story to see and understand key moments where I had been wounded and the things I had come to believe because of them. There were moments of my past that had a huge impact on the man I had become, and I had almost no understanding of how or why. So, for the first time in my life, I was very intentional about looking into my past, starting with my dad, a journey your initiation will require you to take as well.

Let's pause for a few moments because this is such a difficult and sensitive subject. I have seen and been part of many men's introduction to the importance of exploring moments of past wounding. It is rare for a man to easily accept his need for this. For so many men, it feels dishonoring to the most important man in their life. And if the only thing we accomplished in digging into our past was to relive long-forgotten pain and suffering and vilify our fathers, I would agree there wouldn't be any value to it.

For other men, your resistance is coming from a different place. Some of you have stories of significant trauma at the hands of your father. If that is you, let me say this: the things we are about to ex-plore deserve a great deal of compassion and wisdom. As you con-tinue reading and begin the process of exploring your own wounds, I implore you to handle your heart wisely. There is absolutely no room for shame in realizing that you may need help in this battle for your heart. The things I am about to share may be best done with some professional help. As you walk this road intimately with Jesus, receive his tender wisdom for the care of and fight for your heart.

I know and understand that you may be feeling some resistance at this point. So, once again, let's take a moment to extract the precious from the worthless to be clear about the point of all this. First, what we are not doing: this is not an exercise in father bashing. The objective is not to lash out at your father, or mine, and make him a scapegoat for the brokenness, pain, and suffering that has impacted the man you are today. Instead, what you are doing is seeking to understand how the enemy has used these moments to take your heart captive. What you are doing is learning to fight this enemy to take back what is yours. Your dad is not the enemy, Satan and his legion of fallen angels are.

That being said, we have already talked about the extreme of blam-ing Satan for everything and creating a convenient way of shirking responsibility. So while we aren't here to bash and shame your dad or mine, you will have to allow yourself to feel the full weight of the wounding. In my case, my dad took that check from me, his nine-year-old son. Was the enemy influencing his thinking in that mo-ment? Most certainly. Does that mean he bears no responsibility for that? It does not. He made that choice in a moment of weakness, and it proved to be a very significant wound for me. So while the objective is not to lash out and bash our fathers (even for those who experienced abuse and trauma from your fathers), in allowing yourself to feel the full weight of these moments, you can expect to feel some very deep and strong emotions—some that may take significant time to process.

The truth of this becomes even more apparent when you realize there isn't just one moment to which Jesus wants to lead you. My story and yours include several moments that need Jesus' healing touch—and not just for wounds from our dads. I will have more to say about that as we go on but, for now, it is important to know that you will find yourself walking intimately with Jesus to many different moments that proved to have a significant impact on your heart. In my case, it took years to fully process the emotional fallout from these journeys into my past. Yes, years! By no means was this the only moment of wounding to which Jesus would lead me. Not surprisingly, it was a process that strained my relationship with my dad.

It can be a long and difficult road. You will relive very impactful moments and feel rejection, betrayal, diminishment, loss, sorrow, hopelessness, and anger. In other words, you will grieve. Which is exactly where you will find Abba waiting for you.

But you, God, see the trouble of the afflicted; you consider their grief and take it in hand. The victims commit themselves to you; you are the helper of the fatherless (Psalm 10:14).

This is a hard place to stay. I know the things I wanted to do as I started to walk this road. I wanted to dismiss much of it as insignificant. I've thought this, and I've heard this, often: "Yeah, that happened, but it wasn't that big of a deal." Remember, however, what you now know about the bigger story. It is in these moments that Satan used the sacred relationship between father and son to take captive a part of your heart and rob you of your sacred identity. He also used and has continued to use those moments to skew your perception of God. There is a reason, for most of us, the best place to start the journey of fighting for our hearts is in revisiting moments of wounding from our fathers. In targeting the sacred relationship of father and child, more so than any other relationship, the enemy can exact a devastating wound and cement very entrenched skewed perceptions of our heavenly Father.

How? Well, in a moment of inspiration after an encounter with a man unaware of this truth, my brother wrote his own "Screwtape letter." As background, *The Screwtape Letters* is a book written by C.S. Lewis. It is a story of a master demon, Screwtape, and his apprentice nephew, Wormwood. The story is told through a series of letters from master to apprentice as he educates and enlightens young Wormwood in the ways of thwarting "the enemy" (God) and the humans he loves so much. It is an extremely enlightening story, and one I most certainly recommend. However, the inspired "Screwtape letter" from my brother, Tyler, is what I want to share here. (Remember, "the enemy" mentioned here is from the perspective of Wormwood and Screwtape . . . so, that enemy is God.)

Wormwood,

I am so disappointed that you let your subject pledge his life to the enemy. We will talk about this when you and I meet next. For now, you have some work to do. Listen to me very carefully: if he starts to see the compassion, delight, affection, and deep love the enemy has for him, you will not only lose him forever, but he will become a formidable foe against our Master's kingdom. But do not fear; there is hope. There has been a proven strategy you can take to keep your subject in line. You must confuse the true face of our enemy toward him. What you need to do is pick someone in his life who fits the following criteria:

Your subject sought the approval, affection, and delight of this person.

This person either never gave that approval, affection, and delight, or only gave it when your subject accomplished something or followed the rules.

This person was so preoccupied with their own unmet desire for validation that they rarely, if ever, showed deep affection toward your subject.

Your subject was never truly secure in this person's love for them.

I believe for your subject the best person would be his father. Here is the work you have before you. You must convince your subject that our enemy is like your subject's father. Let him feel the enemy's approval of him when he is following the rules, or when he accomplishes something. But *never*—and I repeat *never*—let him see and feel the full, unconditional love the enemy offers unless he only gets small tastes of that love, and only if your subject believes he earns it. If you do this, you will maintain control of your subject for many years to come. And if you are good at it, you will be able to use him to turn others away from our enemy as well . . . especially his own children. If you can do that, you may even earn a promotion.

Your Uncle,

Screwtape

Maybe that is a description of your father or, perhaps, your story of wounding is slightly different. Regardless, it absolutely is a big deal. The desire to dismiss your story as insignificant likely is coming from a good heart that wants to protect your father, or from an instinct to protect yourself. But I have seen this play out often enough to know that behind that thought is just a clever play by the enemy. He is using your good heart against you to lull you back to sleep and get you to back away from the fight.

I know the turmoil you're beginning to feel. But don't allow yourself to be duped into backing down. Remember, this isn't, ultimately, about your dad. You have spent a lifetime learning to cope with the brokenness, pain, and suffering from wounds that have impacted your entire life. As necessary as it is to learn to cope, however, there is something we all need much more than that: healing.

That is what the difficult road ahead is leading to—and it is something Jesus longs to offer you. Listen to his heartbreak as he reflects on the reality of people who are not awakened to, or worse, actively resisting their need for healing.

"For this people's <u>heart has become calloused; they hardly hear with their ears, and they have closed their eyes</u>. Otherwise they might see with their eyes, hear with their ears, understand with their hearts and turn, and <u>I would heal them</u>"
(Matthew 13:15, emphasis added).

His heartbreak drips from these words. He cries for your wounded heart, and mine, calloused and held captive; a heart cut off from the life, freedom, belonging, and unconditional love we were made to know. He longs for us to receive healing from him but, sadly, so many of us have closed our eyes. We have settled for the crumbs of simply trying to cope. Why? Because, unfortunately, most conclude that the price for healing is just too high. So here we are, two thousand years after Jesus uttered these words, closing our eyes, shutting our ears, our hearts growing more and more calloused, and our enemy keeping his prize, winning the fight by forfeit.

Furthermore, this unrealized healing is not just a tragic surrender of your own heart, it is also a death blow to your sacred role as a father. You cannot give what you don't have.

Furthermore, this unrealized healing is not just a tragic surrender of your own heart, it is also a death blow to your sacred role as a father. You cannot give what you don't have. Your divine responsibility is to bestow sacred identity to your kids. To do that, you must find the courage to get your heart back, receive the healing you so desperately need, and learn to live deeply rooted in your belovedness. In learning to fight for your own heart, you will learn how to fight for and teach your kids to fight for their hearts. Your kids have the same enemy. They too will have the same fears and face the same intimidation, as they will one day come to realize their own need to fight for their own hearts. They will learn from you what to do.

So, quiet submission can no longer be the response. Instead, there is something else for you to discover. As you follow God deeper into his invitation to initiate you into intimate sonship, you will also discover a strength you may not yet know you have. Believe it or not, the enemy works extremely hard to avoid the fight—because he knows, in the end, if you discover your source of strength that comes from living in deep intimacy as God's beloved son, it is a fight he won't win. Let's acknowledge, then, the fear and intimidation we all know, and let's also decide together that the time has come to awaken to our desperate need for healing, and to step into the fight. The time has come to walk deeply into your story so that you might see, hear, and understand clearly how those wounds have shaped you into the man you are today. Jesus says it plainly in Matthew 13:15: understand and turn to him, and he *will* heal you.

Jesus says it plainly in Matthew 13:15: understand and turn to him, and he *will* heal you.

Courage, beloved son. Courage.

FRONT LINES

Where, then, do we begin? Well, as you may have guessed, there isn't really a prescription for this. This is a time for an intimate encounter with God. Your initiation to intimate sonship has already begun. It started with his invitation to you . . . by name. It continued with you awakening to the reality of a universe at war fighting over the treasure of your heart. You now know and are prepared to engage the fight alongside God to take back what is yours. The front line of that fight will be found by walking deeply into your story to see, hear, and understand wounds that have long needed healing—especially wounds from your father.

You might begin by recalling key moments from your childhood. Capturing your thoughts in a journal can also be helpful. In those memories, what did your dad do? Or, more subtly, maybe think about what he didn't do. Often, wounding occurs in something that was said or done, or, more subtly, what was needed but not said or done. It usually doesn't take long, after beginning this intentional reflection, for a man to have a painful part of his past come to mind. If that hasn't happened for you yet, stop reading and ask God to reveal a memory to you. Ask and then listen. He *will* answer and, with his answer, an important memory will surface.

What has come to mind for you is no coincidence. That, beloved son, is Jesus leading you into battle. He knows exactly where this fight needs to start, and he will be in this with you each step of the way. If you find yourself second-guessing what has been stirring up for you, resist those doubts. Jesus is leading you to your place on the front lines for your heart. Now . . . let's fight.

AND SO IT BEGINS

I absolutely love The Lord of Rings trilogy. There are a handful of movies I will watch again and again, and this trilogy is at the top of the list. One of my favorite scenes is very fitting for where you are now. In the second movie, *The Two Towers,* the evil wizard Saruman has waged a brutal war against mankind and, specifically, King Theoden and the people of Rohan. The movie builds to an epic confrontation at a fortress called Helm's Deep. The people of Rohan have been hunted, tormented, and oppressed at the hands of an enemy that has wantonly killed and pillaged the land. Saruman has King Theoden under a spell, leaving him free to wage his war unopposed.

But all of that changes when the wizard, Gandalf, shows up to break the spell and rescue the king from his captivity. Awakened, the king's first instinct is to try to flee to Helm's Deep. There, King Theoden hopes the enemy will back down as the people of Rohan lock themselves behind stone walls beyond the reach of evil—or so they think. The people are weary, discouraged, and defeated. So they flee in search of safety. But the enemy does not back down. Saruman seizes the opportunity to strike the decisive blow to a people now trapped behind the walls of their own fortress, to wipe out Rohan and leave "no dawn for men." A legion of fierce orcs, whose only purpose is destruction and death, descend on the fortress. Meanwhile, a terrified and exhausted people muster what courage they can to fight for all that they hold dear. It all builds to the peak of tension as the forces of good and evil stand in an eerie silence and await the inevitable first strike that will start the battle. An old man, shaking with fear, loses grip on his drawn bow and the arrow finds a target. The first blow is struck, and King Theoden, through gritted teeth and steely eyes, simply says, "And so it begins."[2]

Already, you have come a long way. It is no small thing to find your way to the front lines in the fight for your heart. Frankly, the enemy is used to being unopposed—a luxury he no longer has with you. Believe me, he is still hoping to crush you with doubt and fear to intimidate you into backing down. Like Theoden, you may have sought refuge behind walls of fear, doubt, and denial, hoping the enemy will back down. He has not and will not. You have come to understand that reality and, like King Theoden, your courage now has you standing face to face with the enemy in an eerie silence knowing a fight is imminent.

Now what?

We begin.

EXPOSING MESSAGES

Let's go back, for a moment, to the story of the serpent on the prowl with an unsuspecting Eve. We looked closely at that encounter and learned something very important about our enemy: how he uses two intertwined lies as his primary weapon of war. Like any schemer, this exposure has and will do much damage to his ability to wage his war against you. No, he won't back down, but your awareness of that has given you the threat of exposing his schemes. But look a little closer at what we did to gain that insight.

> *The serpent was clever, more clever than any wild animal God had made. He spoke to the Woman: "Do I understand that God told you not to eat from any tree in the garden?"*
>
> *The Woman said to the serpent, "Not at all. We can eat from the trees in the garden. It's only about the tree in the middle of the garden that God said, 'Don't eat from it; don't even touch it or you'll die.'"*
>
> *The serpent told the Woman, "You won't die. God knows that the moment you eat from that tree, you'll see what's <u>really</u> going on. <u>You'll be just like God</u>, knowing everything, ranging all the way from good to evil"* (Genesis 3:1-5, The Message, emphasis added).

Remember the two lies that make up the serpent's weapon of war: God isn't good, and you're not good enough. Note, again, the serpent never actually speaks those lies explicitly. He's more crafty than that. He packages the lies in a way that the ideas will be deeply lodged in Eve's heart—not explicitly stated but very much communicated. The ideas were so masterfully planted that Eve found herself ready to do the unthinkable, never realizing the devastating impact the lies were having. They were masterfully buried *within messages: lies not explicitly stated but still very much communicated.*

Allow me to return to my story. Over the years, every once in a while the memory of me standing there holding out my check to my dad would surface. But time had its effect, and the memory became more and more distant and seemingly irrelevant. It would lay dormant for years. Until my crash and burn. I had come to realize with painful clarity just how desperately my heart needed healing. This has been one of many "front lines" to which Jesus led me over the years. The memory is no longer distant, and now, I know, not at all insignificant.

Even now, as I sit with that memory, yes, the first thing I feel is the sorrow of that check being taken. I see myself standing there knowing that what I needed in that moment was for my dad's strength and honor to affirm my heart, reassure my fear, and with pride in his eyes gently push the check, still in my hand, back to my chest. I needed Dad's strength. I didn't get it. That, of course, brings up many uncomfortable feelings: anger, sadness, and betrayal to name a few. I resist the urge to dismiss those feelings, instead allowing myself to feel the weight of it all and—this is so important—to openly express all of it to Jesus. I don't edit it. I don't explain it away. I accept my need in that moment and grieve how it was not met.

But beneath those feelings something else was going on. As I stood there in that moment having handed over that check, I can now see and hear something else happening, subtly, deeply within my heart. The serpent was most definitely on the scene, weaving his web of unspoken but very much communicated messages designed to have maximum impact on my heart: "You can't rely on God to provide. You know your dad won't provide. Your mom is terrified. You should be too. You will always feel afraid." That wasn't all. The messages got very personal: "Your family is failing. If you really cared, you would solve this problem. *Your dad will love you if you fix this. So do something!*" I kept sitting with it, seeing and hearing as deeply into the moment as I could. Then I landed on what I now know to be one of the most impactful messages of them all: "Can't you see what is happening?

If you really cared, you would do something. This isn't going to get better—*it's up to you!*"

And I began to understand that, in that one moment, I was presented with an idea that would silently shape my outlook and life choices for the next twenty-seven years. And in those years I had become a man in desperate search of validation, seeking answers to my deep questions of identity through achievement and the promise of what others would think of and say about me. In one moment between a father and his nine-year-old son, the message "it's up to me" became a theme around which I would unknowingly build my life. To be clear, this wasn't the only time that message was planted deeply in my heart. As I would come to see over time, this was a key theme, among others, working its way into my heart in several impactful moments. I was already inclined to accept responsibility. Now, I could see, my bent for responsibility was the very thing the enemy targeted with his messages. It was a set-up. And with that message, the enemy had me dangerously close to following in Eve's footsteps. He had me right where he wanted me. But striking my heart with that message wasn't the ultimate goal of his scheme. He was scheming to get me to do *something* in response to that message (which is where we will take the battle next). He has done the same things with you.

Back to you and the memory or memories to which Jesus has led you. As you soak in the details of those moments, the memories will likely begin to stir up your own emotions. You will relive the pain and sorrow and, like me, your instinct may be to resist that. But your fight

> In one moment between a father and his nine-year-old son, the message "it's up to me" became a theme around which I would unknowingly build my life.

starts there: submit yourself to feeling the weight of emotion that has never truly been grieved. As you sit with those memories, what was being communicated to you in those moments? What "reality" was being presented to you? If you could put words to what was not said but still very much communicated, what would those words be? Those are the messages that came through the wounding. Look deeply into what you were feeling in the moment. Allow yourself to feel it all again and name those feelings! Are you trying to edit them and explain them away? Resist that. Instead, turn and offer all of it, unedited, to Jesus, who has been waiting with great anticipation for this beautiful moment. Know that he will not be offended or disgusted; there is no condemnation in this sacred space

> Know that he will not be offended or disgusted; there is no condemnation in this sacred space with him.

with him. After all, he already knows the unhealed emotion that has hardened into a calloused shell around your heart. That shell gets broken when you finally submit to letting it all go and allow yourself to experience the intimacy of grieving with Jesus. This is what it looks like to turn to him and be healed.

SETTING EXPECTATIONS

These are huge steps. In taking this on, you are walking intimately with Jesus to push back and begin to free your captive heart. But I want to be sure I'm not leaving you with the impression that this process is quick and easy. In sharing my story, I summarized in one paragraph what, in reality, took years to unfold. So let me offer a little perspective from my own experiences with this process to be sure your expectations for your own journey are grounded in reality.

First, this is a back and forth, iterative kind of process. I know my description has been quite linear: first this, then this, then this. I can offer that description because, with the benefit of seeing this play out over such a long period of time, I can see how, over time, there was an overall progression. In the trenches, however, the grieving process is quite messy. Memories would surface, bringing about emotions. I would identify messages which would bring about more emotions. The emotions would take some time to process. Some time would pass, and the emotional turmoil might settle for a time only to surface again later for some more intimate processing with Jesus. Sometimes it would all feel a little overwhelming, and I would find it difficult to find the capacity and will to work through it. Which meant that it would take time for me to work through things like the anger, bitterness, pain, and sorrow that surfaced.

It is likely going to take time for you as well. This is a lot to absorb, especially if these ideas are new to you. I don't offer these things with the expectation that it will be fully understood with one reading. Understanding comes through the practice of venturing into our stories and engaging the healing process. You may well want to come back to these pages several times as you continue your journey.

Which also brings me to a word of caution. This can be where some of you will get stuck: losing sight of why you are submitting to all this in the first place. It is for the promise of healing. Jesus asked the question of a crippled man who had been slowly dying inside for thirty-eight years: "Do you want to get well?" (John 5:6). *Why* would he ask such a seemingly insensitive question? Because Jesus can long for healing for each of us all he wants. But he also knows that, unless we also want it for ourselves, his desire alone isn't going to change a thing for you and me. So, yes, grieving is a messy process, something you cannot force or speed up. But it can be a bit of a trap without a regular reminder of what you are moving toward and a definitive answer to Jesus' question. A question very much meant for you and me just as much as that crippled man. "Do you want to get well?" Healing is available for all who answer yes, and you may very well find that your battle includes answering that question regularly. Maybe even, at times, daily.

As for my story, I mentioned before that there were parts of my grieving process that took years to work through. But I was committed to getting well. I did want the healing that Jesus promised. I had much to learn (frankly, still do) about letting go and allowing him to carry those things for me. I was learning to move toward forgiveness, to accept, as author John Eldredge says, that the cross of Jesus was and is enough. We will have much more to say about forgiveness, but for now, just know that my grief was leading me to choose to forgive— even on days I didn't feel like it. It was a process and, even though there were times it felt like it would never end, I can still remember the moment where it dawned on me that where there had once been bitterness, anger, sorrow, and pain, I was now experiencing something else: peace. The deep wells of emotion that had been burdening my heart and straining my relationship with my dad were washed away. Healing does come.

> I can still remember the moment where it dawned on me that where there had once been bitterness, anger, sorrow, and pain, I was now experiencing something else: peace.

Which leads me to share one more observation about my dad. Since Dad wounded me by taking my check when he could not adequately provide for our family, the most predictable way that might have impacted me would have been for me to react by choosing to become focused on a highly lucrative career, becoming an 80-hour-a-week workaholic, sacrificing much in exchange for providing financial security for my family. But that is not what happened. I did at one point believe I could find salvation through a high-paying career field, and that was one of the factors that drove my decision to study engineering. One reason I didn't take the predictable path to being a workaholic, though, is simply because it's just not my personality. But something else very important prevented me from falling into the trap of making financial security an all-consuming idol.

That something was, ironically, a positive legacy that my Dad gave me. As I mentioned earlier, the most wonderful thing he offered me as a kid was his time and presence. He was at my ballgames and school events, we played catch, and he helped me with my homework. He was always supporting me and cheering me on. The importance of that was woven deeply inside of me, just as the wounding became woven inside of me. I knew that I wanted to be as present and available for my kids as my dad had been for me. Just as we are wounded by our fathers, adding to the current of negative generational momentum, most of us also receive wonderful gifts from our fathers that can produce positive generational momentum. Exploring moments of wounding by our fathers in order to understand their impact and pursue healing does not need to feel disloyal to them because it does not negate the important positive legacies they gave us as well.

Back to your journey. Jesus is initiating you into intimate sonship with him: a process that unfolds—no surprise here—by learning to walk intimately with him through this fight for your heart. However, you are not to—nor were you ever meant to—fight this battle alone. You are learning what it is to be a son, to be fathered. This is how he is fathering you. As he fathers you, so you will learn to father your children.

You may not know it yet, but in submitting to grief, choosing forgiveness, and identifying messages, the enemy is now seriously exposed. You are on the verge of a serious advantage in this fight. You are about to do much more than resist the enemy. You are ready to understand his critical weakness. One that, decisively struck, will send him retreating in defeat.

Next: You have fought valiantly and courageously walked deep into a painful memory. Against your instincts you have relived the moments and allowed yourself to feel the full weight of emotions the memory evokes. Now we are going to look at and expose the endgame of our enemy's scheme.

Chapter Six

CRITICAL WEAKNESS

From that time on Jesus began to preach, "Repent, for the kingdom of heaven has come near" (Matthew 4:17).

Jesus answered them, "It is not the healthy who need a doctor, but the sick. I have not come to call the righteous, but sinners to repentance" (Luke 5:31, 32).

How would you respond if I asked you this question: "Do you honestly believe God likes you, not just loves you because theologically God has to love you?" If you could answer with gut-level honesty, "Oh, yes, my Abba is very fond of me," you would experience a serene compassion that approximates the meaning of tenderness.
—Brennan Manning[1]

If there was ever a time I held the power to disappear, this is when I would have used it. There I stood, in front of about seventy-five people on a Sunday morning, all my worst fears being realized. By this point,

I was well aware of the difficulties I was having keeping up with the demands of ministry and, now, it was all about to catch up to me. It was my turn to preach again. But this time, as I began preparing, absolutely nothing came naturally or easily. I continued to grind away, but it felt like I was getting nowhere. The approaching deadline didn't help as my anxiety increased with each passing day. I was down to just a matter of days, and I feared that what I had prepared to that point was, frankly, entirely inadequate. So I worked harder. After all, people would be there to hear what I had to share about God's Word! But as much as I wanted to deliver something powerful, meaningful, and maybe even life-changing, something had happened that simply was not going to change in the short time I had left. I was spent. Utterly and completely spent. I was bankrupt emotionally, spiritually, creatively, even physically. I was working on this sermon to the point of exhaustion and, as I'm sure you've guessed by now, had nothing to show for it.

Sunday came and I did my best to put on a brave front as I began. Almost immediately, though, the feedback from the crowd confirmed my worst fears. As the minutes went on, it only got worse. So there I stood. Bankrupt. Exposed. A sea of disapproving eyes now looking back at me. I had the honor of the pulpit and had failed in spectacular fashion. I wanted to run and hide, but there was nowhere to go. All I could do was stand there in my shame and do my best to finish the debacle with some shred of dignity. I remember the helplessness and hopelessness I felt as I walked off that stage. In my heart I knew this was the beginning of the end. The end of what? Well, in the moment, I thought it might be the end of my days of preaching. But I also had a sense that this could ultimately be the end of the dreams I had to one day be lead pastor of this new church we had given so much of our lives to starting.

My sense of that moment would prove to be accurate. It was, indeed, an end. But it was even more of an end than I had anticipated. In the weeks and months that followed, my wife and I would come to realize our need to leave the church altogether. What I could not see at the time, though, was how my spectacular crash and burn was also the beginning of the end of something else: my enslavement to the tyranny of an illusion that had slowly but surely been squeezing the life out of my heart and soul.

I know. Between my stories and the memory to which Jesus has led you, this has all been a little, well, depressing. We have been venturing into some dark places, some uncomfortable memories. But as King David said:

> *Weeping may stay for the night,*
> *But rejoicing comes in the morning* (Psalm 30:5).

It is true that we live in the reality of a universe at war. And it is true that, with war, comes loss, brokenness, failure, despair, and grief. But that isn't the whole story. Not even close. There is so much more, and our ventures into these dark memories are leading to something extraordinary. I had mentioned my crash and burn before. In the immediate aftermath of that fateful Sunday, and the fallout over the next several weeks and months, it felt like things just kept going from bad to worse. Naturally, it felt like punishment to me. However, at the time I was unable to see what was really going on.

A rescue.

The same is happening for you. As you have walked deeper into God's invitation for your own initiation, you can perhaps relate to that same sense of things going from bad to worse. But hang in there. A rescue is happening for you as well. Though it may feel like it at times, our enemy is not invincible. Far from it. Already, you have become a formidable threat to him simply by learning to oppose him. But we can do so much more than simply oppose him. With a well-placed, decisive blow, you can turn the tables, take the fight to him, and send him retreating in defeat. And you will never be the same. But to do that, you must know where and how to strike.

CRITICAL WEAKNESS

In the climactic scenes of *Star Wars: A New Hope*, the rebel forces have assembled to face down an enemy wielding the most powerful weapon ever made. The aptly named Death Star has the power to literally blow up entire planets. It is an intimidating threat to say the least. But the ragtag assembly of rebels stands in brave opposition nonetheless. At great cost and loss of life, the rebellion first learned of the possibility of a catastrophic weakness built into this formidable weapon and then managed to secure the sensitive information that gave them all they needed to know to destroy the ominous threat. In the scenes before the climactic battle begins, the rebels assemble for a briefing where they all look deep into the design of the weapon and, together, come to understand its critical weakness, how to find it, and, most importantly, their plan to successfully hit the target. Yes, they would have to fight and win many battles along the way to get that opportunity. But as important as those battles would be, they were only victories that would be necessary to get to the one target that ultimately mattered.

You too have started learning to fight and win necessary battles. But so far, as necessary as those battles were, it was all so you could fight your way to the one target that ultimately matters. From the beginning, the enemy has waged a war to exploit your critical weaknesses. He has targeted your sacred identity with lies about God and lies about your worthiness. Uncovering moments of wounding and the messages communicated in those moments have been critical steps in opposing an enemy that isn't accustomed to pushback from you. As you have exposed his schemes, you have taken steps to safeguard your heart and the story he has been exploiting. Most importantly, as you have started the pushback, you have also enabled the healing process to begin. As great as all that is, though, it gets much better. It may surprise you to know that our enemy has a critical weakness too.

AGREEMENTS

The messages you have worked to identify were definitely an essential part of the enemy's schemes. However, as difficult and painful as those messages were by themselves, the enemy still had not achieved his ultimate goal. It may seem subtle, but there is one last element to his crafty plan. In the wounding and the messages, he lured you deeper into his trap until all that was left was for you to, unwittingly, agree with his lies. John Eldredge talks about this concept of making agreements in his book *Waking the Dead:*

> Satan is called in Scripture the Father of Lies (John 8:44). His very first attack against the human race was to lie to Eve and Adam about God, and where life is to be found, and what the consequences of certain actions would and would not be. He is a master at this. He suggests to us—as he suggested to Adam and Eve—some sort of idea or inclination or impression, and what he is seeking is a sort of "agreement" on our part. He's hoping we'll buy into whatever he's saying, offering, insinuating. Our first parents bought into it, and look what disaster came of it. But that story isn't over. The Evil One is still lying to us, seeking our agreement every single day.[2]

This brings us back, once again, to that fateful moment between Eve and the serpent. Please take one more look at Genesis 3:1-7, but allow me to highlight verse 6.

When the Woman saw that the tree looked like good eating and realized what she would get out of it—<u>she'd know everything!</u>— she took and ate the fruit and then gave some to her husband, and he ate (The Message, emphasis added).

As we have worked to "know our enemy," learning more every time we look deeper into the story, we have further exposed his schemes. The intertwined lies that God isn't good and you're not good enough were packaged in messages tailored for maximum impact to Eve's (and Adam's) heart. Prior to their encounter with the serpent, they never had any reason to even *think* about their worthiness or God's goodness and trustworthiness. It had never crossed their minds that they were somehow inadequate or that their life with God was lacking. Eve and Adam enjoyed a relationship with each other and with God exactly as it was designed to be. All of that was seriously threatened with the devastating messages the enemy struck deep into their hearts. The message for Eve that she could be so much more and have so much more was so compelling to her that she was on the verge of doing something that just moments before was unthinkable. It was so compelling to Adam that he stood idly by Eve's side as the serpent lured her deeper into his trap. As devastating as those messages were, though, the enemy still had not achieved his ultimate goal. There was one last element to his scheme. Moments before, Eve never would have contemplated what she was about to do. What changed? What was it that made the unthinkable become irresistible? Look once again at verse 6 for that answer.

First, though, in verse 5 we see the enemy suggesting that Eve could be so much more: just like God, knowing everything! In verse 6 we are allowed to enter Eve's thoughts. In a flash, something changed. The message led her to the trap. She agreed with the message. Upon agreeing, doubts about God's goodness and trustworthiness went from a suggestion to something she now accepted as reality. Adam agreed too, doing nothing to confront the growing threat. So the lie took root and, despite the devastating consequences they had been warned about, they did the very thing God told them not to do. Eve took and ate the fruit and gave some to Adam as well. This was the endgame of the enemy's scheme: luring Adam and Eve into the seemingly insignificant act of *agreeing* with him.

Eve agreed with the idea that she simply wasn't enough. She agreed that she could be and could have more . . . much more. She agreed with the notion that God was holding out on her by trying to keep her

> So she reached for the fruit and, in an instant, got what she wanted: to define good and evil for herself. She also got a devastating whirlwind of heartbreak, regret, and despair.

from that and, therefore, could not really be trusted. Conveniently, she had an option in front of her that, she agreed, had the promise of taking matters into her own hands and fixing all of that. So she reached for the fruit and, in an instant, got what she wanted: to define good and evil for herself. She also got a devastating whirlwind of heartbreak, regret, and despair.

It really is a hard thing to look at. The serpent found a new way to wage his rebellious war against God. Where direct and open rebellion had failed, crafty manipulation of what God loved most would prove to be wildly successful. By shifting his target, he had found a way to strike a devastating blow to the God he hated and the human beings God cherished.

On one level, I look at this story as a bystander, like I'm watching a movie. As Eve reaches for that fruit, inside I'm screaming, *Noooooo!!!!* I feel the despair and bitter sorrow as she gives some to Adam and they eat. And I sit in disbelief as I watch the rest of the scene play out.

Immediately the two of them did "see what's really going on"
—saw themselves naked! They sewed fig leaves together as
makeshift clothes for themselves.

When they heard the sound of God strolling in the
garden in the evening breeze, the Man and his Wife hid
in the trees of the garden, hid from God.

God called to the Man: "Where are you?"

*He said, "I heard you in the garden and I was afraid
because I was naked. And I hid."*

*God said, "Who told you you were naked?
Did you eat from that tree I told you not to eat from?"*

*The Man said, "The Woman you gave me as a companion,
she gave me fruit from the tree, and, yes, I ate it."*

God said to the Woman, "What is this that you've done?"

(Genesis 3:7-12, The Message).

Moments before we were invited into a beautiful story of God creating. And that story of creation comes to a climax as he tenderly crafts mankind and we learn that all his work was done as an outpouring of love for the crown jewel of that creation: humanity. He lovingly crafted them as image-bearers, reflections of himself. He gave them purpose and belonging. Everything was as it was designed to be.

I can only imagine, then, just how deep the pain was for God as he confronted Adam and Eve.

"Did you eat from that tree I told you not to eat from?"

Perhaps it wasn't so different from how we feel when losing a loved one. Human language simply doesn't have words powerful enough to capture emotions that deep. I wonder if Adam and Eve hid, in part, because they hoped they might be able to avoid being confronted with that grief. But it could not be avoided. Still, Adam tried to at least deflect the pain and grief. He was quick to throw Eve under the bus—and subtly blame God at the same time—as mistrust was growing between them. Crestfallen, God next turns to Eve with another haunting question:

"What is this that you've done?"

The story continues, and it doesn't take long to see everything spiral out of control as humanity and creation are collectively consumed by the evil that is now spreading like a cancer.

I may want to look at this story as a bystander. But I can't. It is my story too. Like Eve, I was lured in with the idea that I could be more. I was compelled by the idea that I wasn't enough and that my "ordinariness" was something to be ashamed of and overcome. So I climbed mountains believing that impressive achievement would bring the praise and adoration I was convinced I needed to stand before God and man unashamed. Wounding opened the door to the messages. Agreement with those messages compelled me to shape my life accordingly. You've done the same.

> It doesn't take long to see everything spiral out of control as humanity and creation are collectively consumed by the evil that is now spreading like a cancer.

Adam and Eve's story is our story. It is a very bleak picture. We have all been caught up in the serpent's schemes and co-opted into his rebellion. It is an insurmountable curse, a chasm between God and the humans he loves . . . unless something changes.

And all of this unfolding from a simple agreement.

WE NEED A HERO

The picture of creation and humanity in the aftermath of that encounter is dark. It seems hopeless. The story of human brokenness and failure continues but, alongside that reality, something else begins to emerge. Hope blossoms as God reveals his plan to rescue mankind. Bit by bit, we see God working through fallible, weak, selfish, and shortsighted men and women to fully expose what should have been obvious: humanity's desperate need for a hero that could somehow break the curse and free mankind from the tyranny of the enemy.

As the story continues, this hero slowly comes into focus. A messiah would come. And he would be unlike any hero before or after. An ordinary man . . . a "suffering servant" (Isaiah 53:4-6).

I don't pretend to understand all that happened in the spiritual realm when Jesus was crucified. But I know this: you and I were powerless. We were in hopeless captivity, never to find our way back to God and Eden—unless something changed. You, me, all of us were in desperate need of help! Which is exactly what Jesus came to do. He came to break the curse. He was blameless yet, somehow, took all the blame for us to the grave. Our rebellion and failure deserved punishment; they were a debt that demanded payment. It was a hopeless trap until that debt was paid—a debt paid, in full, by Jesus. Why? So that we might be healed and freed!

This is no passive, disinterested God. For you and me, he is the suffering servant. In the face of the enemy, this is Jesus: fierce warrior, liberator, champion. I don't know how it all worked. I just know it did. The proof that it worked always comes back to one thing: death couldn't hold him. He came back to life. He lives! He lives now. He lives today. He reigns and has authority over all, including the entire realm of darkness. Which means that Satan no longer has the authority to hold us captive—unless we agree to let him. Jesus shook Heaven and Earth when he walked out of hell holding the keys to our freedom. It meant that all the enemy had left, his only hope for keeping us from stepping out of captivity and into freedom with him, was to keep mankind invested in a false reality, to keep us in agreement with an illusion.

The ultimate reality is that we are tenderly, fondly, and affectionately loved, that we belong, and that we have nothing to prove. It is not, however, what most of us experience, and it is not how most of us live. But we can. This is where we start turning the tables. Satan took Adam and Eve captive the moment they agreed with him. He has taken your heart captive through agreements as well. But the most profound truth of Jesus' work is this: the agreement can be broken. What had once been Satan's checkmate in his war against God and humanity is now his critical weakness.

BREAKING THE AGREEMENT

Which brings me back to that inspiring moment of triumph when Jesus walked out of the pits of hell that Easter Sunday holding the keys to our freedom. The work was done. It is done. Freedom is real. It is, in fact, the ultimate reality! But all of us have lived our lives under the tyranny of an illusion.

This is the pivotal issue. Your initiation into intimate sonship is about an awakening. To this point, the work you have done has, bit by bit, been exposing the illusion. But that is only one part of the story. It is not enough to simply see what you are being freed from. It is simultaneously about understanding what you have been freed for. There is a word for this simultaneous action of "turning away from and turning to." Unfortunately, it is a word that requires some effort to recover because, for so many, it has taken on some very negative baggage. It is a word that Matthew says sums up Jesus' message whenever he preached:

From that time on Jesus began to preach, "Repent,
for the kingdom of heaven has come near" (Matthew 4:17).

Jesus himself says his purpose is to call humanity to repent.

Jesus answered them, "It is not the healthy who need a doctor,
but the sick. I have not come to call the righteous,
but sinners to repentance" (Luke 5:31, 32).

Repent!? I don't know about you, but when I hear that word I can't help but picture the guy on the street corner with that wild look in his eyes frantically telling passersby to repent because the end is near. Or I can hear the fire and brimstone preacher thumping his Bible as he exhorts the flock to "Reeeepeyant!"

It has become a word loaded with the baggage of shame. It is so often used like a spiritual club as a command to "get your act together, loser!" It beckons us to feel ashamed for how repulsive we are to God. It paints a picture of a God who, at best, is tolerating you but doesn't really want anything to do with you outside of what he might be obligated to do—if you could just get it together and stop being such a pitiful sinner, spiritual zero, loser, ingrate, and perpetual mess-up. In other words, the word has come to be a source of messages, none directly stated but all very much communicated. There it is again: you're not good enough and God's not really good.

Yet repentance is the core message of everything Jesus preached. Which means that none of that comes even close to what he meant when he said "repent." For Jesus' listeners, his message was a hopeful invitation. The original word used by Matthew and Luke was a word that meant a simultaneous turning from one thing and turning toward another. And it was *always* a turning toward something better. It literally meant "think again." Unlike that wild-eyed man on the street corner, people were *drawn* to what Jesus had to say. Crowds grew bigger and bigger as people who were used to hearing how much they disgusted God got a very different message from this carpenter from Nazareth.

In hearing Jesus' call for them to repent, they were hearing, many for the first time, an invitation to reject the messages of unworthiness. Instead, they were, amazingly, invited to turn toward a God who was calling them home. Yes, Jesus was telling them to turn from their sin. Their sin? Agreement with the enemy! Agreement that they weren't worthy of God and that he wanted nothing to do with them unless they got their act together. The call to repent was a call to break the agreement, to reject the illusion and turn toward the open arms of a Father who never gave up on them and never, ever stopped loving them. Far from a message of contempt and shame, repentance was the central theme of Jesus' teaching because it is from the heart of a God calling his sons and daughters to come home to his outstretched arms.

Jesus did for us what we could not do for ourselves. He went to the cross and paid the price for our freedom . . . in full. That is no illusion. That is the great and ultimate reality. However, as much as he paid and as deeply as he desires freedom for us, it is not something he can or will choose for us. It is the wisdom of his question to the crippled man at Bethesda: "Do you want to get well?" Healing and freedom is already won for all who say yes. Having dealt with Satan, he turned to finishing what he started. Rescuing his sons and daughters and leading them to receive the freedom he'd already won.

> However, as much as he paid and as deeply as he desires freedom for us, it is not something he can or will choose for us.

To this point, everything you have done in the fight for your heart has you poised to exploit what is now, because of Jesus, the enemy's critical weakness. Everything the enemy has done to wage war on your heart was designed to achieve one thing: an agreement. His entire scheme now depends on keeping you invested in the lies that compelled you to agree in the first place. As long as the agreement remains, he retains his claim.

What he doesn't want you to discover is the truth of just how tenuous his claim is. The moment you awaken to the reality of your freedom and break the agreement—the moment you and I repent—we shatter the illusion and turn to the ultimate reality. Successfully strike at the agreement and, like the Death Star, his scheme comes undone. Successfully strike at the agreement and you will recover a piece of your heart and your sacred identity. Successfully strike at the agreement and you will discover what God has been up to all along: a rescue.

It is surprisingly simple. Satan's critical weakness is exploited every time we break an agreement. That being said, just because a thing is simple doesn't mean it isn't profound. Nor does it mean it is easy to do. The enemy will not go quietly. You may now know what the critical target is in the fight for your heart, but it's not enough to just know what the target is. It is a target that will take some resolve to strike decisively, something that cannot be done without rejecting the one thing the enemy has left: illusion. That, beloved son, is a bit more difficult.

Next: When you live a lifetime under the oppression of an illusion, it takes time to unlearn the lies that compelled you to agreement in the first place. Now let's take some time to know our God and, as we do, discover what might be standing in the way of receiving healing, love, and freedom.

Chapter Seven

JUST WHO DO YOU THINK YOU ARE?

"But the father said to his servants, 'Quick! Bring the best robe and put it on him. Put a ring on his finger and sandals on his feet. Bring the fattened calf and kill it. Let's have a feast and celebrate. For this son of mine was dead and is alive again; he was lost and is found.' So they began to celebrate" (Luke 15:22-24).

As I write this chapter, I'm just beginning to come out of a prolonged funk. It wasn't that long ago that I was enjoying an extended season of joyful intimacy with God. But, slowly, that steady flow of life began to dry up. Looking back, I can trace the moment things started to change to the end of summer. At first, I just dismissed it as the natural ebb and flow of life. Fall brings a lot of changes. Most of the changes for us were what almost every family goes through as the kids start school again. It's usually a very familiar transition but, this year, not so much. It didn't seem like much at the time, but there was one factor that made the start of this school year different. This year the kids actually started the school year by . . . going to school. It sounds funny to say, but, of course, I'm referring to the radical impact of the COVID pandemic that altered every facet of all our lives for well more than a year. So, on the one hand, it is so good to see "normal" things like kids going back to school. But for me, personally, as the world continues its return to full speed, I'm feeling the impact of that in ways I hadn't anticipated.

I know for many people the shutdown of the world because of the COVID pandemic was a difficult, even traumatic, ordeal. I understand the financial, mental, spiritual, and social challenges people faced—not to mention the trauma of COVID itself. While we experienced some loss as well, I think I was very much in the minority in that the quarantine turned out to be a very good thing for me and my family.

As the reality of the quarantine set in, I was no different than just about everyone else; it was a difficult new reality to adjust to. But something began to happen as the days went on. The radical and surreal halt to the sprint of daily life offered a contrast between what I had known as "normal" and the abundant and lavish flow of peace, joy, and wholeness I was now experiencing in the "new normal." As days turned into weeks and weeks into months, I found myself breaking free from chronic busyness. Suddenly the demands of daily life and the ever present pressures of things I felt I should be getting done and places I was supposed to be all stopped. It was like the world granted me permission to just "be." It was awkward at first, but there was time to simply listen to birds, watch the sunrise from my deck, read books, watch movies, play games with the family, ride my bike, golf, journal, talk with friends, paint and remodel rooms in the house, fix things that had been neglected for years, fish with my sons, share music and books with my daughter, and enjoy long walks and cooking with my wife. Those were all things I had enjoyed before, but the big difference was the gift of enjoying it all without some nagging thought about what I "should" be doing instead. It was a time of deep intimacy with God and joyful, carefree presence with the people I love.

The contrast turned out to be a massive exposure of how pervasive the illusion of "normal" life was! I now saw more clearly than ever just how much meaningful life "normal" busyness had kept me from experiencing. I'm not sure I would have seen past it so clearly without such a radical worldwide shutdown. It was such an enticing and hopeful glimpse into a life freed from the tyranny of constant activity—activity so pervasive that even when we weren't "busy," it was still occupying part of my heart and mind. I had no idea just how much of my capacity to be present was consumed by what I once assumed was "normal." I knew, though, that the day would come when the world would return to full speed. And don't get me wrong. Just like everyone else, there were things my family and I were looking forward to doing again. But I now also knew that there were things I very much wanted to hang on to. We had been given a gift. And I had every intention of preserving it for me and my family.

Until I didn't.

Over the summer, the world did start to return to full speed. Early on, we eagerly took the opportunity to reconnect with people we hadn't seen through the quarantine. My youngest son had been missing interaction with his friends, so we were looking forward to play dates, birthday parties, and sports activities. We went to the movie theater and took vacations to reunite with loved ones. It was inevitable, even good, that some of our former busyness began to return. But as summer ended and school began, our family ramp-up gave way to a little more here, a little more there. It was subtle. I could feel the effects on my heart and soul, but it was incremental, and slowly disorienting. Bit by bit, what had been a prolonged time of intimacy, peace, joy, and growth started to dry up. In its place was isolation and a slow and steady depletion spiritually—and then physically. Even though I wanted to be vigilant, I still got swept up by a world that had started sprinting again. Why? Because I never said no. I didn't want to miss out. I didn't want to disappoint someone. There were opportunities to do things we loved and had been missing. There was always a good reason that made it easy to overlook what was happening to my heart. Busyness had made a comeback and, despite my good intentions, I had completely whiffed on my desire to guard against its intrusion on my permission to simply "be." How could I miss something so completely that I had been intentionally watching for and guarding against?

It swept in under cover, disguised by an old agreement. The problem wasn't the things I said yes to. It was that I said yes to everything—good things. A retreat, a day at the ballpark with my brother, flag football for my son, in-laws up for the weekend, a family gathering at an apple orchard, a college football game. It was so good to have these kinds of things available again. Like everyone else, we missed them. So having those opportunities felt like a gift. It seemed like we would find life in the experiences, especially because we'd been deprived of it for so long. But the non-stop sprint at which we were taking it all in took it from a loving gift to a barrage. I wasn't receiving the moments. I had started consuming them. In the process, my extended season of carefree intimacy with God slowly dried up.

During the quarantine, all my "nos" were said for me. As I'm coming to understand what happened, I now see clearly that I have much to learn about saying "no" for myself. That feels very hard to do sometimes. It's an old agreement rooted in the idea that joyful moments and great experiences are scarce, that such good things only come my way sparingly, so I'd better take in every opportunity that comes along. If I dig down enough, that thinking reveals a perception of God as a reluctantly stingy source of good things—an idea wrapped in my old agreement that "it's up to me" to find and secure good things for me and my family.

It's an illusion.

And it's pervasive.

ILLUSION

My initiation into intimate sonship started with my crash and burn and began well more than a decade ago. I was learning, for the first time, how to fight for my heart and push back against the enemy's schemes. I was learning to receive and experience the ultimate reality of my belovedness. I was learning to live lighthearted and carefree, bit by bit shedding the burden of trying to prove my worthiness. I started learning it then. I'm still learning it today. I'll continue learning it the rest of my life.

Over the years I have come to appreciate a key milestone for people in their own initiation journeys. Appreciate isn't the right word. It's actually a sacred moment, a time when someone awakens to and understands the promise, hope, healing, and freedom of their belovedness and, in understanding, also realizing just how hard it is to receive. For many of you reading and following along with your own initiation journey, that is exactly where you are. It is a sacred moment God fathers his beloved sons and daughters into again and again as he ushers us ever deeper into healing and freedom. These are the moments that shake Heaven and Earth because it is the first step back home.

But it also can feel like a stalemate. It is one thing to see the critical weakness of the enemy. The idea of breaking agreements is not a difficult concept to grasp. But, often, it is extremely difficult to actually do. Breaking an agreement is a decisive act. It is a simultaneous rejection of the agreement and receiving of the kingdom of God. Receiving. Resting. Knowing. Experiencing . . . that you are loved, you belong, and you have nothing to prove. The more any of us understand that an existence like that is available, the more we want it. Why, then, is it so hard to receive?

In a word, the barrier is illusion. There is a disconnect between the promise of belovedness and the reality of our everyday experiences. Every one of us is born into a world that relentlessly squeezes us with variations on the intertwined lies of the enemy. We know what Jesus accomplished. We understand its implications. But we have this lingering issue of the reality we live in—that your worthiness of love and belonging is up to you to prove and secure. That your value depends on what you do or don't do, have or don't have, and what others say or don't say about you.

Our enemy is relentless in his assault, always pressing and swarming us with that illusion. It is just as we discussed in the last chapter: it's all he has left. He is desperate to keep us so preoccupied with it that we never have a chance to see past it. It may be a false reality, but, practically speaking, that makes little difference to you and me. If it's all we've ever known, calling it a false reality does nothing to dispel the very real experiences of living daily in that falsehood.

In the classic movie *The Shawshank Redemption,* a beautiful story of human dignity is told through the lives of two men: Andy Dufresne and Ellis "Red" Redding. As Andy and Red navigate life under the tyranny of a crooked warden and a soul-crushing prison system, a brotherhood grows. Their story is told through the narrative eyes of Red. His grizzled wisdom is perhaps most poignantly shared through one particularly sad chapter of the story. One of the men in their brotherhood, Brooks, had been a Shawshank prisoner for fifty years, carving out a niche for himself as the prison librarian. His story takes an abrupt turn when he is finally, and unexpectedly, granted his parole. He had spent the vast majority of his adult life in prison. Now an old man, he would taste freedom again. This was no gift, though. Brooks did his best to adjust to his new reality. But, in the end, it proved to be more than he could handle. Brooks wrote a note to his brothers in Shawshank, mailed it, went back to his apartment, and committed suicide. He had his freedom, but, without the support he needed to make that transition, the freedom was a curse. As the men of Shawshank tried to make sense of what happened, Red offered this keen insight:

> He's just institutionalized. . . . The man's been in here fifty years, Heywood [the prisoner Red is addressing]: fifty years. This is all he knows. In here, he's an important man, he's an educated man.

Outside, he's nothin'—just a used-up con with arthritis in both hands. Probably couldn't get a library card if he tried. . . . These walls are funny. First you hate 'em, then you get used to 'em. Enough time passes, it gets so you depend on 'em. That's 'institutionalized.' . . . They send you here for life, and that's exactly what they take. The part that counts, anyway.[1]

That's us. Institutionalized. We were designed for the freedom Jesus won for us. But we're used to the walls, to the illusion crafted by the enemy to keep us blind to the reality of our freedom. Or, if he can't keep us blind to it, he presses the illusion even more fiercely to keep us from receiving it. Author John Eldredge says it like this:

Life has a way of eroding our confidence in the goodness of God. What a ridiculous understatement; let me try again. Life is a savage assault, striking at random, poisoning our heart's assurance that God is good, or at least good toward us. This makes it so hard to find more of God, to receive him in fresh and wonderful ways into our being. So it's here we must seek healing, and now is a good time to do so.[2]

Yes, that's it. We need healing. Now is a good time for it.

ANTIDOTE TO THE ILLUSION

The antidote to the illusion is healing. This is where all that we have explored—wounds, messages, agreements, *everything* we have uncovered to "know our enemy"—leads us. The illusion is all the enemy has left. The enemy fears a man or woman who has awakened to the existence of the illusion. He is absolutely terrified of a man or woman who tastes life with God outside the illusion. Yes, the critical weakness for all of that is the breaking of that agreement. But you and I are institutionalized. You know a free life exists and is available. You want it. You know that the enemy has lured you into agreements that have given the illusion life. And, now, you also understand that his tyrannical oppression of your heart is tenuous. It all unravels the moment you break an agreement. But breaking the agreement involves turning from and rejecting the illusion and, simultaneously, receiving the ultimate reality of intimate sonship with God. The illusion must be dealt with.

Brooks needed healing. He needed care and support to unlearn the institutional reality of Shawshank that had become his life. And he needed to relearn the life of freedom outside its walls. He didn't get what he needed. Fortunately for you and me, we have an Intentional Father who knows exactly what we need and exactly how to usher us back to the freedom that is our birthright. He knows that all of us need healing, a process that can take some time.

It's very much like the process I have gone through to fix my golf swing. Once I learned what a good and true swing felt like, it took (and is still taking) time to unlearn years and years of bad muscle memory so I could then, at the same time, relearn new muscle memory that would allow me to more consistently repeat the "true" swing. This is exactly what God was doing to father me in my early days in the wilderness every time I was asked about my vocation. Every single time I answered, I was forced to confront the shame I felt about answering "I'm a stay-home dad." I would be asked, I would answer, and then I would be forced to deal with the fallout. Each time I had to choose what I knew was true but still had not come to truly experience: that I was loved, that I belonged, and that I had nothing to prove. I just wasn't going to unlearn a lifetime of illusion overnight.

Yes, it was a false reality, but it was the only "reality" I'd ever known. So the question kept coming. I kept answering. I kept squirming. But something else was happening. Every time I was asked, I was forced to decide how I would answer. It was a choice between taking a stand and claiming the ultimate reality of my belovedness in spite of the shame I felt, or giving in to the shame by finding a way to deflect and hide. Bit by bit, with the repeated choice to take my stand and answer, the walls of the illusion were slowly being chipped away. Every time I was asked and I chose once again to answer, I was striking at the agreement—and I was being healed. The illusion was breaking down, undone by a thousand blows. It would take months of this exercise before I would experience the ultimate reality of my belovedness. Then, one day, it happened. I was asked and I answered . . . without shame. I felt the warm embrace of my Abba as he tenderly spoke deep into my heart: "Welcome home."

It was my initiation into intimate sonship with God. For the first time I had tasted and experienced the ultimate reality of what Jesus accomplished for me. It was the dawn of a new life of intimacy with God. There was, and continues to be, so much more he has for me. I needed healing then. I still need it today. Here I am, more than ten years later, and I'm still learning to break free from the illusion. Daily, in fact. My initiation into intimate sonship was only the beginning. And it is only the beginning for you. We do, after all, live in a universe at war. The enemy is desperate to keep us from our freedom. So he swarms us daily with his lies designed to keep us invested in some version of a false reality built around the two deadly lies: God isn't good, and you're not good enough. These are the walls we're used to. But that is beginning to change.

Jesus knew all too well the challenge his sons and daughters faced in receiving the freedom he'd won. He knows that we are institutionalized. And he knows that we need healing as an antidote to the illusion. Healing is a challenging topic to explore without sitting elbow to elbow and heart to heart with someone. If we could be together, I could hear your story, I could share more of mine, and the uniquely personal experiences that make up the story of your life would also tell the story of the healing God has for you. There is a great deal of mystery and extremely intimate "knowing" in the healing Abba offers. It involved a months-long process of answering a question I dreaded. It was painful but, I now know, it was straight from the heart of my Intentional Dad, who knew exactly what I needed to heal. The process of healing will be just as unique for you. And as your life of intimate sonship continues, the healing will continue to be a beautifully unique journey with him. But that doesn't mean there aren't some things common to all healing journeys.

We have all built and lived out the stories of our lives under the influence of the illusion of those two deadly lies. But our stories are unique. So, yes, the healing you need and the process of healing will be a unique experience for you. However, healing begins with two things that are essential, and common, to every healing experience: healing our perception of God, and healing our perception of ourselves.

HEALING OUR PERCEPTION OF GOD

Jesus loved stories. It was one of his favorite ways to teach. His parables were powerful and relevant illustrations that always impacted his listeners profoundly—and still do. There was one story, though, I believe he told to take direct aim at the illusion. Healing is the antidote to the illusion. And the healing we need starts with healing our perception of the Father. The Prodigal Son is a story told by Jesus to do just that. It is a brilliant story of a man and two sons that is filled with unexpected twists. The "surprises" in this story challenge our perceptions of our heavenly Father so that we might see past the illusion into his true heart. We have spent a significant amount of time working to know our enemy. Let's turn now to knowing our heavenly Father's true heart that we might begin to see him as he truly is.

The story Jesus told is simple enough. There is a man with two sons. Apparently, the younger son grows restless, and the promise of adventure in a distant land is irresistible. He finds life at home with his father and brother lacking, so he takes a bold step:

> "*The younger one said to his father, 'Father, give me*
> *my share of the estate*'" (Luke 15:12).

Apparently, there was no affection or love toward the father from the younger son except for what he could obtain from his father. It is an offense, an insult, but the young man is undeterred; he asks for his inheritance anyway. Having obtained the resources he needs to break free from his father, the younger son sets off to find the life he'd dreamed of.

> *"Not long after that, the younger son got together*
> *all he had, set off for a distant country and there*
> *squandered his wealth in wild living"* (15:13).

Not surprisingly, the bottom fell out. So far, this is strikingly familiar to the story of Adam and Eve. It's not stated directly, but the younger son had clearly found his life with his father lacking and had made an agreement that he believed could net him more—much more. He also made an agreement that what he wanted could be found "in a distant land." Having made the agreements, the promise of life in that far-off land became irresistible. He longed to get away. So he did what he believed he had to do. He demanded, and got, his wealth. Again, Jesus doesn't say it directly, but it is not hard to imagine how much this hurt the father. The father gave the son what he asked for anyway, allowing his son to learn for himself the shortsightedness and foolishness of his plans.

> *"After he had spent everything, there was a severe famine in that*
> *whole country, and he began to be in need. So he went and hired*
> *himself out to a citizen of that country, who sent him to his fields to*
> *feed pigs. He longed to fill his stomach with the pods that the pigs*
> *were eating, but no one gave him anything"* (15:14-16).

He left in search of adventure and life. But it was a road that ended in, for a Hebrew, the lowest place imaginable: a pig sty. Hungry, alone, and desperate, the young man reached bottom when he found himself longing to eat the pig slop. He was finally bankrupt. His journey began with the confident belief that he knew how to find and attain the desires of his heart. As he stared longingly at that slop, he'd finally reached the end of himself. The illusion of self-rescue had, finally, been fully exposed. Destitute and broken, his thoughts finally turned back to his father. He knew the damage he had done and, naturally, assumed that bridge had been burned. But it was the only choice he had left. So he began to prepare his speech.

"When he came to his senses, he said, 'How many of my father's hired servants have food to spare, and here I am starving to death! I will set out and go back to my father and say to him: Father, I have sinned against heaven and against you. I am no longer worthy to be called your son; make me like one of your hired servants'"
(Luke 15:11-19).

That sounds about right. No longer worthy to be called his son. It would be a tremendous act of kindness for his father to just count him among the servants. It was the best he could hope for. At least, that's what he thought.

But this is where things take a very unexpected turn. The young man does return home. However, far from the contempt, scorn, and shame he'd prepared himself for, this happens:

". . . while he was still a long way off, his father saw him and was filled with compassion for him; he ran to his son, threw his arms around him and kissed him" (Luke 15:20).

Wait. *What?* The father saw his son while he was still a long way off? That means he had kept a vigilant watch! Why? Well, what we might be expecting is that the father is watching closely for his son's return so justice can be done, so that the Father can drop the hammer on him. But, shockingly, we couldn't be more wrong. Far from an angry, vengeful Father, amazingly, Jesus says that the father was "filled with compassion for him"! How can this be?

The surprises aren't done! Filled with compassion, the father *runs* to meet his son, *throws* his arms around him in an emotional embrace, and *kisses* him. This is all so very unexpected. Yet every twist was a brilliant exposure of something Jesus knew all of us desperately need healing for. The fact that we are surprised at the Father's responses is precisely the point of the story! It is a brilliant exposure of the way the illusion distorts our perception of him—an illusion that the younger son, in spite of his father's radical responses, still had a hard time seeing through. So he started his speech:

> *"The son said to him, 'Father, I have sinned against heaven and against you. I am no longer worthy to be called your son'"*
> (Luke 15:21).

Again, the father's response is completely unexpected:

> *"But the father said to his servants, 'Quick! Bring the best robe and put it on him. Put a ring on his finger and sandals on his feet. Bring the fattened calf and kill it. Let's have a feast and celebrate. For this son of mine was dead and is alive again; he was lost and is found.' So they began to celebrate"* (Luke 15:22-24).

Where we expected the younger son to return to his father's contempt and scorn, instead we see the father eagerly run to and embrace the son he had been vigilantly watching for. But the emotional embrace was only the beginning. Far from throwing his son in among the lowly servants, he honored him with a robe, ring, and sandals! Instead of vengeance, there was a raucous feast and celebration. The younger son could not have been more wrong about his father. We have been too.

But Jesus still wasn't done exposing the illusion. There was an older son too. Upon his brother's return, he is perplexed and hurt by his father's behavior. No, that's not strong enough. He was livid.

> *"The older brother became angry and refused to go in.*
> *So his father went out and pleaded with him. But he answered his father, 'Look! All these years I've been slaving for you and never disobeyed your orders. Yet you never gave me even a young goat so I could celebrate with my friends. But when this son of yours who has squandered your property with prostitutes comes home, you kill the fattened calf for him!'*
>
> *"'My son,' the father said, 'you are always with me, and everything I have is yours. But we had to celebrate and be glad, because this brother of yours was dead and is alive again; he was lost and is found'"* (Luke 15:28-32).

What do we make of this? On the surface, it seems the older son has a point. He did everything he was supposed to do. It was the younger son who abandoned them and ran off to squander everything on wild living. The older son remained at his father's side, never "disobeying" him. In other words, he did everything right. Yet the party is thrown for the younger son? How does this make sense? Believe me, Jesus' listeners were just as perplexed. The father's behavior just doesn't compute. But again, this is precisely the point of what Jesus is teaching here. It doesn't make sense because the things we expect to happen in the story are things that "institutionalized" humans expect. The sons, both of them, related to their father based on the illusion that his primary concern, the number one thing he cared about, was their behavior.

Wait.

Don't rush past this.

I'll say it again.

The sons, both of them, related to their father based on the illusion that his primary concern—the number one thing he cared about—was their behavior.

But this is an illusion.

And it is pervasive.

The younger son ran in search of life because he felt nothing with his father; he was apparently disillusioned with the perceived demands of cold, relationless obedience. And then, when his situation became so desperate that he had to return home, he expected to be received harshly based on his truly despicable behavior. The older son, on the other hand, remained obedient. So, upon learning of the party thrown for his brother, the older son became incensed. He had lived under the assumption that his life of cold, dutiful obedience had earned him a favored status with the father. When that assumption proved to be wrong, the older son felt betrayal. What he didn't understand was that he was, in the end, no different than his brother. *Both sons completely missed the father's true heart.* While their responses were different, the illusion that shaped their relationship with the father was the same. Both were relating to their father believing his number one concern was their dutiful obedience. They both perceived their own value and worth through the lens of their behavior. The younger son assumed his poor and foolish decisions disqualified him from a relationship with his father. The older son thought his dutiful obedience had earned his father's favor. *What they both missed was the father's true heart: the thing that mattered most to him was not cold, relationless obedience but instead a deep intimacy with his boys.* Healing our perception of the true Father is to see the Father as he is, to see his true heart and look into his eyes and see the face of compassion: a gaze of delight, adoration, and love from your true Father who longs for deep, uninhibited intimacy with you.

Ironically, it was the younger son who would finally see the father's true heart. The older son, it would seem, never saw through the illusion. And, therefore, he never truly understood his father or experienced the intimacy his father longed to share with him.

HEALING OUR PERCEPTION OF OURSELVES

We are no different. Jesus knows just how pervasive the illusion is. He knows what the illusion has done to our perception of our Intentional Dad, and he knows what the illusion has done to our perception of ourselves. Our desperate need for healing is no different than the men and women who were there when he told that story. The healing we need starts with healing our perception of God, which, simultaneously, opens the door to healing our perception of ourselves. And as we receive healing for how we perceive ourselves, we find ourselves living more and more fully in the ultimate reality of the Father's true heart toward us.

We all have a bit of both sons in us. Like the younger son, the illusion has swarmed us with a perception of God as a "cosmic stiff"—a stingy taskmaster constantly looking over our shoulder to keep us in check. He is constantly keeping score, and any mess-up is sure to be met with disappointment, disgust, contempt, and, most likely, punishment. It is an oppressive "reality" to live in. So, like the younger son, we've gone in search of something better. We have taken what God has given us and looked for life in what we do, what we have, or what others say about us. It is my story. It is your story. Perhaps you

> We all have a bit of both sons in us. Like the younger son, the illusion has swarmed us with a perception of God as a "cosmic stiff."

went looking for life in career, education, reputation, or title. Perhaps you sought solace in adventure, parties, or women. The younger son ran in search of life. He did it to get away from a father, it turns out, he did not know. We've done the same.

The older son tried a different approach. Instead of running from the "cosmic stiff," he decided to build his life around appeasing his father. Cold, dutiful obedience was his calling card. He did all the right things at all the right times. His "religious" life, so he thought, stood in stark contrast to that no-good, wayward brother of his. With that contrast, not only did the older son imagine that his dutiful obedience appeased the father, he imagined that it had earned him status as the "favored son." The older son is part of our story as well. We find ourselves preoccupied with comparison, keeping a vigilant watch on our behavior—and that of others. It is hard to admit, but there is a perverse sense of comfort that comes from a nameless, faceless sea of humanity that is "far from God"; a humanity that is, by comparison, much farther away than I am. The flip side of that, of course, is the crippling realization that my best attempts to appease may be inadequate . . . a reality the older son within us is eager to ignore.

Can I be bold for a few lines? The world of religion is filled with "older sons." I point it out, though, not simply as a general statement. Notice in the story that Jesus never tells us more about the older son. The story ends with a cloud of strain between him and his father. If the story had been told as expected, the father and the older son would be the ones partying together. For Jesus' listeners then, and for us now, it is really difficult to reconcile. For some, it proves to be too much to accept. The truth, though, is that all of us have some of the older son in us. I do. You do. And he is stubborn. He needs healing just as much as the younger son—probably more. Why? Because if he were to be asked "Do you want to get well?" he would likely give you a contemptuous, bewildered look with a question of his own: "What do you mean, 'get well'?" Healing is the antidote to the illusion. But the older son has such a hard time healing because he simply does not believe he is in need of it. Right now, his perverted perception of God is rewarding him with a sense of being favored. There is a word for this trap: religion. What is religion? It is any system in which we ask, and answer, what it takes to appease God: to perform, behave, and achieve to please God and earn his approval. *Any* system.

Pick any world religion, and this is the central premise. The endless lists of do's and don'ts, shoulds and oughts, should not's and ought not's become the cold, relationless measuring stick by which our worthiness is judged. Perform well and receive your reward of praise and perceived favor with God. Underperform and receive the shame you "deserve." We know the world of religion well. But here is where I offer an idea that will be difficult for some of you. The life of Christianity as commonly experienced is a life of religion. Yes, Christianity, for so many, is a religion. This is such an important issue. It is the central issue Paul discusses with the Galatians. And he has extremely strong words about the trap of religion, calling it the equivalent of slavery (Galatians chapter 5). And that is exactly what it is.

The Prodigal Son, in my experience, is a story most often explored through the character of the younger son. But the older son is no less significant. Again, I think Jesus told this story to take a shot at the illusion and offer a glimpse into the healing we all need around our perceptions of the Father and of ourselves. It was his heart to bring that healing to his listeners then, and it is his heart for you now. It may be hard to accept, but it is such a relief for all who do.

My story certainly includes some of the younger son. It includes even more of the older son. Whether you responded by becoming a rebel (the younger son) or a brown-noser (the older one), the illusion behind it was the same. It has robbed you of knowing your heavenly Father as he wants you to know him. And it has robbed you of knowing yourself as he wants you to be known.

I'll be honest. It is difficult for me to know how, at this point, I can help you swim in these deep, healing waters. It would be so much easier for me to share a cup of coffee with you where I could look you in the eye and help you grasp and experience the healing available right now. And it is so important that you do. This is the central foundational issue, the pivotal truth that is the heart of your initiation journey. I have been searching, then, for words that might help you go from being aware of what is available to receiving it.

Perhaps a question is just the thing: *Just who do you think you are?*

The healing of our perceptions of God and our perceptions of ourselves is an invitation to shed all pretenses, to lay down all the ways the illusion has driven us to institutionalized answers. Those answers may be different for each of us, but the illusion behind it all is the same. So, then, how do you answer that question? That isn't just a rhetorical question. Because the way forward comes when we are finally, mercifully free of every answer except one.

That one answer? Well, first let me invite you to see a little more clearly ways you might think to answer that question. As I was praying, thinking, and searching for how I might do that, I came across this "Opening Word" from Brennan Manning for would-be readers of his book *The Ragamuffin Gospel*. Like me, he wanted his readers to be as prepared as they could to receive God as he is and, in so doing, receive the truth about who they are. His words also seemed relevant for us right now. So I offer Manning's wisdom here and invite you to take his invitation for the readers of his book as the same invitation for you to examine how you perceive yourself:

This book is not for the super spiritual.

It is not for the muscular Christians who have made John Wayne, and not Jesus, their hero.

It is not for academics who would imprison Jesus in the ivory towers of exegesis.

It is not for noisy, feel-good folks who manipulate Christianity into a naked appeal to emotion.

It is not for hooded mystics who want magic in their religion.

It is not for Hallelujah Christians who live only on the mountaintop and have never visited the valley of desolation.

It is not for the fearless and tearless.

It is not for red-hot zealots who boast with the rich young ruler of the Gospels, "All these commandments I have kept from my youth."

It is not for the complacent who hoist over their shoulders a tote bag of honors, diplomas, and good works, actually believing they have it made.

It is not for legalists who would rather surrender control of their soul to rules than run the risk of living in union with Jesus.

If anyone is still reading along, *The Ragamuffin Gospel* was written for the bedraggled, beat-up, and burnt-out.

It is for the sorely burdened who are still shifting the heavy suitcase from one hand to another.

It is for the wobbly and weak-kneed who know they don't have it all together and are too proud to accept the handout of amazing grace.

It is for inconsistent, unsteady disciples whose cheese is falling off their cracker.

It is for poor, weak, sinful men and women with hereditary faults and limited talents.

It is for earthen vessels who shuffle along on feet of clay.

It is for the bent and the bruised who feel their lives are a grave disappointment to God.

It is for smart people who know they are stupid and honest disciples who admit they are scalawags.

The Ragamuffin Gospel is a book I wrote for myself and anyone who has grown weary and discouraged along the way.[3]

Men, if we would see into the face of our heavenly Father, if we would behold his heart as it truly is, we would also see ourselves as we truly are. *Just who do you think you are?* You are a man who is battered, broken, tired, discouraged, and lonely: hands bleeding from the weight of the heavy suitcase of shame, fear, and self-doubt. You are an ordinary man who gets bored, scared, impatient, tired, confused, and defensive. You can be arrogant, proud, and stubborn. You can lose your temper, be shortsighted, become very selfish. You also have known success, growth, and sacrifice. The years have left you older and wiser . . . and keenly aware of just how much you have yet to learn. It is your story, and it is mine. Yet none of that gets us to the ultimate reality of who we truly are. Because we are also relentlessly pursued, fiercely defended, infinitely loved, and passionately treasured by a God who has never, ever been deterred by your ordinariness or mine. Nor has he been "won over" by our accolades, intelligence, talent, achievements, or obedience. His heart for you has never been and never will be rooted in cold, relationless obedience or a demand for performance. See through the illusion and behold your true Father: a God who, through all the good and bad, ordinary or extraordinary, failure or success, has *always* fiercely and relentlessly pursued you with an unquenchable passion for intimacy.

He knows how the illusion has perverted your perception of him. Break the agreement and reconnect with the Father who has never stopped his vigilant watch for your return. Break the agreement and turn to the Father, filled with compassion, sprinting toward you now. You are not your faults, your brokenness, and your weaknesses. Nor are you your achievements, accolades, or your possessions. You are not a rebel disqualified from the loving embrace of the father, nor are you a "golden child" secured by your good behavior. Turn to the Father as he is, receive his emotional embrace, and you will begin to find yourself.

So: just who do you think you are?

Break the agreements, and you will learn for yourself what Jesus has known all along: you are loved, you belong, and you have nothing to prove. You are God's beloved son!

That is, and always has been, more than enough.

Welcome home.

Next: The true heart of the father has always been defined by a fierce desire for intimacy with his beloved sons and daughters. Invitation is an integral part of an intimate life with God, and he always has one for you.

Chapter Eight

INVITATION

I'm absolutely convinced that nothing—nothing living or dead,
angelic or demonic, today or tomorrow, high or low, thinkable or
unthinkable—absolutely nothing can get between us and God's love
because of the way that Jesus our Master has embraced us
(Romans 8:31-39, The Message).

"Be sure of this: I am with you always, even to the end of the age"
(Matthew 28:20, NLT).

"Never will I leave you; never will I forsake you" (Hebrews 13:5).

I was inside playing as I heard the commotion outside Grandma's house. There was no mistaking the excitement in my mom's voice—excitement any five-year-old simply had to explore. So I ran outside and there it was: a huge delivery truck . . . and my Dad walking toward me with a big, knowing grin on his face. At the time he was working for a restaurant supply company as a delivery truck driver. Like any five-year-old, I was fascinated with big machines. So when Dad pulled up in that truck, my eyes grew wide with awe. Still, the best was to come because he didn't just stop by to show me his big truck. He also came with an invitation: to ride back with him on the final run of his day. I could hardly believe it as he scooped me up in his strong arms, opened the door, and lifted me inside. I may have just been a little boy at the time, but I felt like a king.

It is such a joyful memory for me. In that moment, my dad stirred up something divine. His invitation called out my belovedness. . . and more than forty years later, I have no trouble at all remembering what that felt like. Yes, everything about the truck was exciting. But my heart swelled because of Dad's invitation to join him. He didn't have to say a thing. I felt loved, adored, and treasured. My dad wanted me with him in a moment just for the two of us. It is the kind of love and delight every child is made to want and need from their father—and we never grow out of it. The desire is divine.

When we are young, we look to our parents to satisfy that desire. That is a good thing. It is the design. It is also the design that, on our journey to adulthood, our parents would teach us, prepare us, and train us to receive that sense of sacred identity from the primary source. This is the intentionality of initiation, and this is the divine responsibility God has invited you into as a father. It's why you picked up this book in the first place. But it may not have been what you expected because, to this point, we have spent almost no time discussing your fatherhood. Instead, we've focused entirely on your sonship. Why? Because you cannot give what you don't have. And in order to understand God's design for fatherhood, each of us must learn, first, to be fathered sons. You'll remember, then, that everything we have explored together so far began with an invitation to do just that. It is the pattern of fatherhood. Our heavenly Father invites. We respond and move toward the invitation. Then, as we are fathered, so we father our children. Your life of intimate sonship with God, then, is the strength and source of what you now will begin to offer your children. The pattern always starts with an invitation.

This is why it is so important that we find healing for our perception of our heavenly Father. Until we begin to know his true heart toward us, his invitations will hardly be, well, inviting. As our perception of our heavenly Father heals, we begin to see that his invitations are about what he wants *for* us and not what he wants from us. Our Intentional Dad is always inviting. Living a life of intimate sonship with him is a life of seeing those invitations and moving toward them. No, his invitations are not all easy things to move toward. But they are always good. It is how he fathers us and, in so doing, teaches us to father our children.

With that in mind, let's explore some of these open invitations, what it looks like to move toward them, and, in so doing, what it looks like to invite our kids to do the same.

BEHAVIOR

AS I FATHER YOU . . .

All right, let's start by picking up where we left off in the last chapter. Before we dig in, though, let me start by acknowledging the challenges that come with talking about behavior as something God wants his sons and daughters to look at with him. In fact, let's be more direct than that. We are talking about sin. This is another word, like repent, that has a ton of baggage. Why? Here again, it is a word dripping with shame. This is one of those things that can be difficult because we can't help but see this through the cloud of the illusion. It feels like an invitation to get beat over the head with condemnation as we sit and face all the ways we don't measure up. No thanks!

So, here again, we have some extracting to do. The word sin simply means "to miss the mark." In the simplest sense, then, sin is a word that points out something most of us already know to be true: we miss the mark. We miss the mark in seeing our heavenly Father as he is. We miss the mark in understanding and living from our sacred identity. We miss the mark in our failure to love others well. For most of us, it's not hard to acknowledge. Still, the mere mention of the word evokes anxiety, fear, and defensiveness. So, yeah, saying this is an invitation is like saying you're invited by your dentist to get a root canal. Still, it is an invitation, and one our Intentional Dad simply will not allow us to ignore. It is not an easy invitation. But it is good.

The root of the fears is a skewed perception of the Father. We have been missing his heart for us and, in the process, missing his invitation and what he wants for us. The true heart of the Father has always been defined by a fierce desire for intimacy with his beloved sons and daughters. He has never been interested in or moved by cold, relationless obedience. However, this doesn't mean that he doesn't care about how we live. In fact, he cares deeply because how we live has a profound impact on our intimacy with him and our relationships with others. His invitation to look at our sin, then, is not to condemn, but to heal and free us.

For God did not send his Son into the world to condemn the world,
but to save the world through him (John 3:17).

God does have an awful lot to say about humanity. Not all of it is flattering. In fact, most of it is not. It doesn't take a biblical scholar to find any number of examples of God's devastating assessment of you and me.

"My people are fools; they do not know me. They are senseless
children; they have no understanding. They are skilled in doing evil;
they know not how to do good" (Jeremiah 4:22).

The Lord says: "These people come near to me with their mouth and honor me with their lips, but their hearts are far from me. Their worship of me is based on merely human rules they have been taught" (Isaiah 29:13).

As it is written: "There is no one righteous, not even one; there is no one who understands; there is no one who seeks God. All have turned away, they have together become worthless; there is no one who does good, not even one" (Romans 3:10-12).

Ouch.

The reality is, we all have a part of us that, like Eve and Adam, very much desires to be our own god. Each of us is broken, desperate, and needy. We are compelled by the promise of self-rescue and the desire to be the center of the universe. To say that it is a part of us actually isn't strong enough. It is much deeper than that. Arrogance, pride, and narcissism are undeniable realities of our humanity, cancers that threaten to consume each and every one of us. The story of humanity is quite ugly. It is an ugliness you and I have an amazing capacity to participate in. So, no, it is not at all flattering. But it is true. And make no mistake, God is very aware of it, cares deeply about it, and, in fathering us, invites us to look at it with unvarnished clarity.

Nobody enjoys this kind of truth-telling. But just because it isn't fun or comfortable doesn't mean it isn't loving. Author Peter Scazzero says it like this:

The critical issue on the journey with God is not "Am I happy?" But "Am I free? Am I growing in the freedom God gave me?"[1]

This is a good time to expand our concept of love. Love, in our modern culture, has come to mean something very nice but, I'm afraid, also something very incomplete. There are aspects of love that we prefer to focus on: kindness, gentleness, acceptance, and compassion to name a few. These are all such good things, all things we are learning to see in our heavenly Father as our perception of him heals. While we hang on to all of that, though, we must also understand that love is far more sophisticated than that. True love—love that heals, restores, and frees—also includes things that maybe we'd rather run from: truth-telling, discipline, and, yes, suffering. God's invitations for us are quite often found in the middle of things we instinctively want to run from. We miss those invitations because we are preoccupied with being happy. It's the wrong question. Instead, the central issue is freedom for intimate union with the Father. There are things about each and every one of us that are unflattering, harmful, destructive, and rebellious. When the Father looks at you and me, he sees all of that, and he most definitely does not pretend otherwise. Healing begins when we see it as clearly as the Father does.

What, then, is so inviting about all of this? In a word, freedom. How we live has a huge impact on our intimacy with him. His invitation is to look with piercing clarity into the issue of sin so that we might "turn to him and be healed" (Matthew 13:15). So he invites you and me to see the ugliness for what it is, to see what is true. Then he invites us directly into it with that ever-present question: "Do you want to get well?" How does he invite us? By offering to explore with him why we live the way we do. And by inviting us to ask important questions of ourselves.

What was at work in your heart when you exploded in anger at your kids yesterday? Why are you so impatient? What's up with the contempt you feel for your neighbor who voted "the wrong way" in the election? What is it that compels you to stay at work an hour longer than you need to everyday? Why is it that you care so deeply about your salary? Why do you take so much pride in what you do for a living? Where you live? What you drive? Why do you hang on to a career that sucks the life out of your heart and soul? Why has your career become more important than being a dad and husband? Why do you feel anxiety at the mere mention of a meeting with that certain person? Why haven't you talked to your son in two years? Why do you find it so hard to say no? Why do you feel ashamed about your balding head and round belly? Why do you start things but never finish? Why are you so obsessed with health and fitness? Why do you struggle with porn? Alcohol? Drugs? Why do you find it so unsettling that your kid didn't make the travel baseball team? The honor roll? The lead role in the play? What is going on that every other driver on the road is an idiot? Why are you so cynical and jealous toward your brother? Why do you isolate? Why do you try to take charge with everything? Why do you talk about "those people" behind their backs? Why do you feel envy when good things happen for others? Why is it you never forgive . . . ever?

How we choose to live—our behavior—is a massive and ongoing invitation from Abba to look into our hearts with piercing clarity. There is always something behind the behavior that is crying out for healing. There are ungrieved and unhealed wounds, crippling messages, and agreements behind it all. It is an inescapable part of being a fathered son. It is also an inescapable part of being an intentional dad to your kids. It's not enough, though, to simply know that the invitation is essential and ever present. Knowing the true heart of the Father is also essential in extracting the true nature of that invitation from the dreadful experience we all imagine. He invites us to confront sin because he doesn't just see what is true about our condition. He also sees what is most true: our sacred identity as his beloved son. Our hearts cry out to be free. Which is exactly what our Intentional Dad wants for us. His invitation is for freedom from what is true and freedom for what is most true.

The father's heart is not, nor has it ever been, to condemn us with shame. Recognizing this changes everything and has proven to be extremely important for me and my family. My own journey in understanding shame and its impact in my life and the very real prison it had created for my heart began when a friend introduced me to Brené

Brown's book *Daring Greatly*. It is worth your time to read, but for now, let me summarize the core transformational idea she presents. Brown offers a profound distinction between shame and guilt. Shame carries a message aimed directly at our identity. It says "something is wrong with me." It leaves our hearts wide open and vulnerable to the relentless efforts of our enemy to strip us away from our belovedness. Shame compels us to hide from God and from each other. Shame isolates us by convincing us that we are the only ones contending with certain struggles and failures. Shame is the force that fuels the fires of self-hatred, and it is shame that compels us to project that self-hatred onto God, leading us to conclude that, at best, he is mildly disgusted with us.

It is, once again, the illusion. So we need reminding—and lots of it—that even (especially?) in the more difficult invitations, God's heart toward you is good and unshakable. It is exactly what Paul boldly declares in his letter to the Romans: *nothing*—absolutely *nothing*—can separate us from the love of God (8:39). Let that echo in your soul for a minute. Repeat it. Repeat it again! I want to stand on my chair and celebrate every time I read that! Our belovedness is eternally secured. So the perception we have of God looking at us with an air of disappointment and some degree of disgust is simply, amazingly, profoundly, graciously not true.

Intimacy, however, is a different matter. You know from your own experience just how much our intimate connection to God is assaulted. This is what you are fighting for. It is also what your heavenly Father is fiercely passionate about. So, yes, he tells us the truth about our sin because it has a profound impact on our intimacy with him. You know this from your own experience with your kids. You love them deeply. But you also know just how much their behavior impacts your intimacy with them. Really, dads, what stirs inside you when your son or daughter is disrespectful toward you? For sure, it is an experience that, among other things, undermines intimacy. The pathway to restoring strained intimacy with your kids requires dealing directly with the heart issues behind the behavior that caused the strain. So here are a few thoughts to explore for yourself and your kids.

AS I FATHER YOU . . . SO YOU FATHER YOUR CHILDREN

God does indeed tell us about, and compels us to face, the hard message of what is true. None of us can deny that we've missed the mark. None of us are exempt from the diagnosis of failure. And while we may want to ignore those things, growth and freedom simply cannot happen without acknowledging our failure and coming to a place in our lives where we want to grow and gain more and more freedom from it—to "get well." Here is the distinction. Far from looking at us with disgust in the midst of our failure, God never stops seeing us as his beloved sons and daughters. He simply does not cast shame on us. Instead, when we look at our failures from the perspective of our belovedness, we now realize that what we are is guilty. Guilt says that I am responsible for my failures. Guilt says that I recognize the consequences of my failure. Standing firmly in the promise of my belovedness, I do not need to hide as I once again come gratefully, humbly, and confidently to the cross and the freedom Jesus won for me. Guilt says "I did something wrong" or "I have failed." Shame says "something is wrong with *me*" or "I am a failure."

As parents, we put a lot of effort into addressing behaviors. We teach right and wrong. We discipline our children. We coach them. We correct them. We are no stranger to the duties we have to shape behavior and our kids' responsibilities for how they live. It is no different with our heavenly Father. Just as you compel your children to own their behavior, so God does with his children. But his heart for us never changes when he does. Shame and its debilitating messages are never present in Abba's efforts to discipline us. Guilty? Yes. After all, I must own the guilt if I am to be healed, move forward, and grow. But shame? Never, ever, ever.

Here is the thing about shame. The illusion is thick with it. Our daily experience in the illusion includes a daily assault from shame. This is a freedom, then, that I have found I always have to fight for—for myself and my family. It is so easy for the messages of shame to creep in. Anytime there is a need for a "hard conversation" with your kids, just know that you will also have to contend with shame. So, as the years have passed, I have learned to be very intentional about how we deal with such times. When those moments come and our kids need discipline, coaching, or correction, I am always sure to frame what we talk about with the reminder (to my kids and to me) that our family simply refuses to give shame any ground. We make no agreements with shame and reject the enemy's efforts to obtain one. We remind each other that we are talking about and addressing something because they are guilty. We are talking about something they did or did not do. We are working to look beyond the behavior to what is beneath it. It is always a fight for the heart.

We are *not* talking about, nor will we allow any messages to enter the conversation to suggest, that there is something wrong with who they are. We are vigilant about this because the threat to identity is very real, and the consequences are severe. This particular issue of freedom from shame has proven to be one of the most consequential realities for me and my family. The more you understand it and practice it for yourself and your family, you will feel the same way.

VULNERABILITY

AS I FATHER YOU . . .

We had an unusually warm day earlier this month. It's late fall now, so when the weather is that good I can't help but hear the golf course calling me. I had hoped to play my round alone but, alas, I wasn't the only one who heard the course calling. That meant I would be playing with a couple of other men I didn't know. So we went to the first tee box and introduced ourselves. The first man I met told me his name, asked mine, and then immediately told me that it had been close to two years since he'd last played. He wasn't done. He wanted to prepare me. "I'm not very good," he said. The rest of the round we talked about several things. But he was extremely self-conscious about how he was playing and what I might be thinking about it. In other words, he imagined that I was watching with contempt and judgment, and he felt vulnerable. I felt for him and tried to encourage him, but his internal battle continued the entire round. I know that uneasy sense of vulnerability all too well. We all do. In fact, earlier this summer I was paired with a couple of guys, one of whom turned out to be the course teaching professional. He did not do anything to make me feel uneasy, but still I felt that same sense of vulnerability!

Vulnerability is another idea that is very difficult to associate with invitation. That's because the illusion bombards us with shame about our wounds, weaknesses, brokenness, and ordinariness. Shame tells us again and again that those things are proof that something is wrong with us. Through the lens of shame, then, vulnerability becomes *exposure*—and it is certain to be greeted with contempt and condemnation. Let's face it: we all have some painful experiences of being vulnerable with the wrong people. In fact, it's worse. The most painful truth is that our hearts—even our *humanity*—has been mishandled and trampled by people close to us. Already we have spent a lot of time looking at one of the most devastating examples of this: wounding from your dad. Vulnerability feels scary because it is! So we're understandably guarded. We tread carefully and, in some way, shape, or form, make an agreement that we won't open up to anybody. It's safer that way! It's another way that shame torments and cruelly oppresses us. Like Adam and Eve, those humiliating experiences leave us feeling naked and desperate for the nearest fig leaf to hide behind.

We've all gotten very good at hiding. We hide by carefully crafting a version of ourselves that has no cracks, weaknesses, blemishes, scars, or inadequacies. It is our false self that we then carefully maintain as a defense against the threat of shame. John Eldredge calls it the poser. Brennan Manning calls it the impostor. Over the years I have heard it called masks or the pretender. Whatever you call it, it is very much a part of your story. Your false self is reading these words now—and it doesn't like being called out like this. But what if I also pointed out something obvious that perhaps you have been reluctant to admit? Maintaining the image of the false self is exhausting, isn't it? Take a moment to be brutally honest with yourself. How much of your day is spent, consciously or subconsciously, evaluating, comparing, assessing, and adjusting the "you" that you allow people to see depending on their "signals"—or what you might imagine they're thinking? My friend on the golf course was consumed by it and, I'm afraid, it took away from his joy of playing that day. (I had to fight the same thing earlier in the summer.) But that's a minor example. How about staff meetings at work? What happens if you're not a big sports fan surrounded by a bunch of guys reliving Saturday's game? What's it like for you to take on a home improvement project if you're not handy? Maybe you know next to nothing about cars so taking your car in for service is, frankly, terrifying. Let me get a little more pointed. What stirs inside as you look at the perfect life and perfect kids everybody brags about on social media? What stirs inside when you go to church? Do you feel like it would be okay to be brutally honest and open about your struggle with porn, that your marriage is hanging by a thread, that your kids have you perplexed and your wife exhausted, or that you are seriously struggling to pay the bills? Or would it be more honest to say it feels like you're the only one who doesn't have his life together so you double down on the impostor role?

Every one of us has a carefully crafted false self that we have spent a lifetime perfecting. Long ago we made the agreement that vulnerability was way too risky. For most of us, we have been maintaining this version of ourselves for so long we've forgotten who our true self is, and this gets to the heart of this invitation. Vulnerability does not have to carry with it the burden of shame that turns it into exposure. You are learning to live more and more from your sacred identity, which means you are learning to reorient your moment-to-moment, day-to-day living around the ultimate reality that you are loved, you belong, and you have nothing to prove. Shame is constantly assaulting that. It's the illusion, once again, and Jesus is always inviting you to break the agreement and find healing and freedom as you come out of hiding. Vulnerability is simply an admission that you need fathering and a courageous step away from the safety of hiding. Jesus, the one who invites you, knows it's scary.

Here again, though, it is why healing our perception of the Father is so important. Within this invitation he's teaching you to trust him and his heart toward you. His heart toward you is compassionate, gentle, patient, and so very good. You've been misunderstood. Your heart has been missed. Your wounds, and the messages that came with them, taught you to hide. But you no longer need to hide. You no longer need to pretend. You've been spending your life crafting and maintaining a false self that you deemed presentable and, therefore, safe to the world around you. You've been carrying that burden for so long you don't even realize how heavy it has become. What would it be like, though, to lay that burden down? What if you didn't have to pretend to be perfect, to have it all figured out, to always know what to do, what to say, and when to say it? What if you could be more and more free from the oppressive demand for perfect kids, a flawless marriage, and an endless demand to do more, be better, and have it all? What if you could go to work, go to church, or simply play golf and not be completely preoccupied with what someone else may or may not be thinking? What if you could start being authentic and honest about what's really going on in your heart? *This* is the invitation of vulnerability.

How, then, do we do that? By learning to ask and answer a simple question: "How's my heart?" It sounds simple enough, but let me explain a bit more. I have the privilege of sharing life with a group of men who come together once a week, primarily to ask and answer that question with each other. We have met for several years. Most of the men there have been at it much longer than myself. We joke, tell stories, share snacks, and talk football, all the things you would expect a group of men to do around a bonfire each week. But we always get down to the most important reason we come together: to be vulnerable with one another by asking and answering "How's your heart?"

It is funny, and telling, that even though we do this every week, and have for years, every time the question is asked, everyone freezes and goes silent. Each and every one of us feels the fear. Let's face it: trusting the wrong person with our vulnerability can be extremely damaging. So it makes sense, and it is very wise, to take time to discern those in our lives who can be trusted with our precious hearts. The hesitation and fear we experience, each and every time, speaks to just how precious and sacred . . . and fearful . . . the invitation is. By now, those of us who gather each week know it's safe. Still, we all need a moment to break the agreements again. And then we get real. One by one we offer each other our sacred hearts. We speak to what's going on and take turns reminding each other of our sacred identities. We are all on the journey of learning to hear, live, and experience that truth intimately in our lives with Abba. But God also made us to have others around us who know how to fight for one another's hearts. Sometimes it is the simple joy of encouragement that comes from having good friends and allies. Other times we find ourselves in a season of life that has our heart and soul under heavy assault, and vulnerability opens the way for "carrying each other's burdens" (Galatians 6:2). We don't do this to simply dump our problems on someone else. We aren't there to wallow in self-pity, nor are we there to "fix" one another. We all know that we need each other's strength, but we also know that the responsibility for our spiritual well-being is not something to be pawned off on someone else. With that healthy dynamic in place, we are there to move toward God's invitation to vulnerability, to put down the impostor, and to receive the healing he wants for us.

There is something else. One thing we always lovingly, yet firmly, push back on is the mindless response we're used to giving and getting. You know this one: "I'm fine." Don't get me wrong. Often many of us are fine and have wonderful, beautiful, and joyful experiences with God to share with one another. "I'm fine," then, is often true, but this question is an invitation to something much deeper. We lovingly and gently push back on that response because it circumvents the invitation. So when we ask, we know it is a time to truly sit with the question and take an honest and unashamed look at the condition of our heart. Perhaps your heart is alive and carefree and you are experiencing the delight, peace, and joy of your belovedness. On the other hand, as you truly move toward the invitation, there will be times you find something else you've been neglecting to face, and there is more stirring in your heart than you wanted to admit. Or, worse, you have a storm raging inside that you have been furiously trying to keep the world from seeing. It is a hidden life that has been eating you alive. Which is why James, Jesus' brother, tells us:

> *Confess your sins to each other and pray for each other*
> *so that you may be healed* (James 5:16).

You may not yet feel that kind of trust with someone else. I understand the wisdom of cautiously pursuing that. But that is an invitation within the invitation. Start looking for it, and be very intentional about finding it and cultivating it. We all desperately need it more than we want to admit. In the meantime, the invitation is open now to start practicing this with God . . . daily. Personally, I have found the use of a journal to be one of the most effective ways to do that. I answer that question with God by writing; doing this is so good for my heart. You may have a different approach. It doesn't matter, really. What matters is moving toward the invitation and learning to hear the question and answer it. No more hiding. No more pretending.

AS I FATHER YOU . . . SO YOU FATHER YOUR CHILDREN

This is a good time to be clear about something else. There is an underlying risk with all we have explored together in this book. Fatherhood is an institution that, in our culture, is riddled with shame.

As such, it is also an institution hiding behind firmly entrenched false selves. It would be easy to slip into the idea that to be an intentional dad means being infallible and perfect in fulfilling your divine responsibility—or that being an intentional dad simply becomes another mask to hide behind to pretend you are a perfect father. If that is a thought, or concern, or expectation that has been lingering, let me be the first to burst the bubble. This is not, never has been, and never will be a pathway to perfect fatherhood. As much as you may want to avoid it, you are going to have moments of failure. You are still going to wound your kids. You are going to miss their hearts, and you will misunderstand each other. Perfection is not God's design for your fatherhood journey. Vulnerability, though, is essential.

One of the barriers that can come between kids and parents is trust. Vulnerability has been an essential part of the trust our family enjoys with one another. If my kids were ever going to trust me with their vulnerability, I had to show them that I could be trusted. So it was up to me to model vulnerability to my kids. My wife and I modeled it in our relationship with each other and in our relationship with them. I'm not perfect, their mother isn't perfect, and that is something that is very healthy for our kids to know.

It is important, then, to seize appropriate moments to tell them about your own struggles. Ask their forgiveness when you have hurt them or let them down. When you are frustrated or angry, tell them why. Explain what you want for them and how this issue is working against that. Your heart for them is good, even when—maybe especially when—you're angry. Let them know your heart. Tell them about when you were a kid and you made a regrettable choice. When you have something you need to own, model for them what it looks like for a beloved son of God to own his guilt while being secure in his belovedness. If we try to present to our kids anything else, it won't be long before they will, at first, be suspicious and then just plain dismissive. They know better. And if we want our kids to trust us, they have to know that we are also growing and learning. And they need to know this life of intimacy with God is a lifelong journey you are on, and one you are inviting them to join. Let me share one story of what that looked like for us.

My oldest son, Ben, is a teachable and eager learner. As we progressed through the initiation process, he was always eager to listen and learn as we worked together to understand the things God was doing in his life, and what it meant to live into those things. Many of those life moments came out of his experiences as a wrestler. He was a very competitive wrestler from third grade all the way through high school. As you might imagine, there were ample life lessons his wrestling experiences presented. We had many conversations about character. But what I didn't realize right away was just how fixated I had become. In my desire to capture the moments and life lessons at hand, I eagerly pointed out all the opportunities to "live into" the moment and grow his character. We talked about it frequently. That is, until one day when he was about 12, and the weight of it simply became too great for him. In a fateful and beautiful moment, despair in his voice, he said something straight from his heart that I will never forget: "Dad, I know how important this is. And I want my character to grow too. But it just seems now that there is always something wrong with me that I have to work on."

Oof. His words were so beautiful—and jarring. In a moment, I suddenly realized I had been failing him. I had become so fixated on his character growth that I had cut him off from the foundational truth of his sacred identity as God's—and my—beloved son. I had unknowingly compelled him to try growing the fruit of character by communicating to him that if he wanted it enough, he could make it grow. It was religion at its worst: a horrible burden of trying to do enough things right to get God (and Dad) to love him.

His courage and vulnerability stopped me in my tracks. Suddenly I saw just how badly I was missing the mark. And it became one of the defining moments of our initiation journey together. I had hurt my son, and I had done it out of my own brokenness and shortcomings.

I was climbing mountains again and, this time, trampling my son's heart in the process. I had a choice in that moment. I could react to the sense of shame that hung over me and become angry or withdrawn. Or I could take the opportunity to respond to his vulnerability by being vulnerable myself. After sitting with the beautiful sting of my son's truth-telling, I knew what I had to do. I owned my failure, explained to him just how wrong I had been, the damage I'd caused, and the wounds I'd given him. Then I asked for his forgiveness . . . which he gave with a big hug around my neck.

This would not be the only time we would need reconciliation with each other. This initiation journey is not easy and, no doubt, you will have your own experiences of failure and reconciliation. But that failure is not the whole story because we simply refused to give up on seeing this mission through to the end. There were many times that we had to forgive one another, pick each other up, and keep moving forward. The journey will challenge each of you more than you can imagine. You will not get through this without hurting one another. You will have to be teachable, forgiving, persistent, and, above all, vulnerable. So, no, it is not your divine responsibility to be a perfect parent. After all, we are being fathered as we are fathering. Your story is ongoing— just as it is for your children. We never outgrow our need for fathering. Which is why our heavenly Father invites us to be vulnerable. And why, now, you are learning to do the same for your kids.

GRIEF

AS I FATHER YOU . . .

This is an invitation that goes hand in hand with vulnerability, and one you've already been moving toward. We've discussed the painful but necessary process of grief in healing. We live in a universe at war, and with war comes loss, wounds, and suffering. None of us escape this life unscathed. Most of us have lived day to day coping with that reality. God's invitation, though, is to move beyond coping to the healing we truly need. Once again, John Eldredge's observation is so true: "A wound that goes unacknowledged and unwept is a wound that cannot heal."[2] This is another invitation that is hard . . . and messy . . . and so very, very good.

It is also something we don't do very well. We fear the mess and, frankly, the surrender of our sense of control. So we fight and resist this invitation and the wounds go unhealed. We go on with life assuming that, with time, the pain will just fade away. Which is sort of true. The old saying that "time heals all wounds," however, is just plain wrong. Time alone does not heal wounds. Time does distance us from painful memories. But distance is not, and never has been, the same as healing. Instead, it would be much more accurate to say that "time plus healthy grieving heals all wounds." Anything short of that is little more than ignoring and pretending. We may think *I'm over it,* but the heart tells the tale. You may be unaware, but your life is leaking. You've been trying to hold it all in but it comes out in fear, bitterness, apathy, cynicism, withdrawal, busyness, denial, victimhood, depression, control, and more.

You may not want to hear this, but it isn't working.

Here again, your Intentional Dad is inviting you to grieve with him because your unhealed wounds are barriers to intimacy with him. You have already spent some time moving toward this invitation as you've started exploring wounding from your father. It wasn't just your dad, though. There are mother wounds, sibling wounds, peer wounds, disappointments, wounds of loss, and wounds of failure just to name a few. We all have a lot of grieving to do. No, God does not invite us into all of it at once. It's part of the intimate journey of sonship with him, and he will lead you to those seasons of grieving at exactly the right time that your heart is ready. There is a wisdom to the healthy grieving process. It is likely, though, that you've spent a lifetime instinctively resisting that invitation. Now, beloved son, you are learning to move toward it. In my own seasons of grieving, I have found it helpful to be aware of the five stages of grief first brought to the public consciousness by Swiss-American psychiatrist Elisabeth Kubler-Ross:

Denial

Anger

Bargaining

Depression

Acceptance[3]

There are any number of resources available to dig into those stages further, but knowing there is a process and being aware of the different phases has been extremely helpful in understanding my own experiences. But I have learned something else along the way. In your efforts to be intentional with this invitation, I would simply add that the concept of "five stages" implies that the grieving process is linear. It is not. There really is no formula, and there is no controlling it. That's the scary part. But I think it is also what makes it divine. I believe grief is a gift from God intended to be shared with him. It requires surrender and trust, key attributes of a life of intimate sonship. It also requires that we learn to be at peace with the idea that things don't always need to be "fixed." Your story is sacred, and so is the pain that is an integral part of it. You know the pain of being told things like "Everything happens for a reason"; or, "That's nothing compared to what others have gone through!"; or, "God is good all the time!" These naive and shallow cliches are simply deflections from somebody unable and unwilling to sit with difficult and uncomfortable things. And in their shallowness they actually communicate a message of shame and rob you of something sacred. By playing make-believe and simply pretending that a slogan can wash away the turmoil inside, we pay a heavy price. We cut ourselves off from the honesty and authenticity essential to a vibrant relationship with the only One who can bring peace and healing to the pain and wounds we've been living with.

Grief is hard because it requires us to walk into and sit with our pain and suffering. I don't know anybody who is eager to sign up for that. But as much as we try to avoid it, there is also something that comes of the pain and suffering as we move through the grieving process. It is an undeniable truth for me that the times of profound suffering, wounding, and loss have also been the times of my most significant growth. I'm betting that has been your experience as well. The undoing that we experience in suffering is what gives birth to the growth and healing we long for. Richard Rohr says it this way: "The old self always has to die before the new self can be born."[4] Paul had his own way of saying it to the Romans:

Not only so, but we also glory in our sufferings, because we know that suffering produces perseverance; perseverance, character; and character, hope (Romans 5:3, 4).

Vulnerability is an admission that we need fathering. Grieving is his invitation to receive that fathering and the healing we need. Cliche slogans will not do. Let's face it: there are times it feels like God has abandoned us, failed us, and let us down. Our stories are all marked by failure, regret, and the bitter reality of limitations. There are also bigger moments of trauma. Each moment, no matter how big or small, has had a profound impact on us. And there is perhaps none bigger than the impact of our perception of God himself. He's big enough to take all the hurt, anger, and disillusionment of our darkest moments . . . even when we are honest enough to admit anger and disillusionment toward him. Grieving starts when we are ready to be authentic about the storm raging inside. You may have assumed that your anger was offensive and irreverent to God. So you've suppressed it. But remember: he is fiercely passionate about intimacy with you. Your suppression is not honoring him because the result is quite the opposite of intimacy.

Look, God already knows how we feel. Intimacy with him means trusting his true heart toward us and, in trusting his heart, finally finding the courage to be brutally honest about the hurt, disillusionment, and anger you feel. More than that, he cares deeply about the suffering we experience, even the seemingly smaller things we want to dismiss or at least diminish because we assume they are too insignificant for him. When we cut all that off with a trite slogan, we lie to ourselves and to God about the very existence of real anger, hurt, and pain. And what won't be acknowledged won't be healed. God's invitation to grieve is to courageously surrender the sense of control we hang on to by pretending everything is okay when, in reality, it is not. It is the courage to be authentic with God in your pain and faithfully move through the grief with him that leads to the healing he wants for you.

AS I FATHER YOU . . . SO YOU FATHER YOUR CHILDREN

As fathers, we can offer a great gift to our children: model for them and teach them how to be authentic and courageous in grieving. Invite them to be honest and open about difficult circumstances—yes, even if it means being honest about feeling angry toward you or even God himself. As God has fathered me to be vulnerable and authentic with him, so I have worked to cultivate that same level of trust with my children. I want the kind of trust that my kids feel the freedom to tell me when I have made them angry or disappointed them. That is an exercise of vulnerability, and it is good. It is what Ben did when he was 12, and it was a profound moment for both of us.

Much more recently, my daughter, Ellie, and I experienced an equally profound moment. Just a few days ago, the family gathered at the kitchen table to share a weekend breakfast. As we spent time checking in with one another, my daughter took an incredibly courageous step of vulnerability. We are in the midst of a very special season with her as it is the final year of her initiation journey. Well, on this particular morning, she took a very difficult—and most important—step in that journey. She has recently been following God into deeper understanding of her heart, especially as it relates to her emotional life. My daughter has always been someone who experiences a strong emotional life. She feels things very deeply. Growing up, there were many times that the expanse of those emotions would impact the entire family. She was young and tiny. Her emotional life was not. Often, it was difficult for me to know how to respond. I was about to learn that some of the ways I did respond had impacted and hurt her deeply.

Now on the verge of adulthood, God has been fathering her into healing and redemption of this truly beautiful aspect of her personality. What my daughter shared with me over breakfast was her grieving as she has come to see and understand my part in some significant wounding. In one moment, during her freshman year of high school, I delivered a wound that sealed a message of shame about her emotional life. She pointed out that my response to her, often, was to try to "fix" the issue. The message? That something was wrong with her that really *needed fixing*, and that it was something she needed to figure out.

I have to tell you, it really stung to hear her words. Of course, that wasn't what I wanted for her at all. Still, my unhealed brokenness became a source of great pain and wounding for her. It broke my heart to know that I was responsible for such a cruel and oppressive burden of shame that she had been carrying for a few years. And, at the same time, I was so proud and thankful for her wisdom and courage. She discovered the wound by living deeply from her belovedness and responding to God's invitation to father her through grieving the wound so that healing could come. She realized that one of the results of that wounding was a burden of shame, and the fruit of that shame was, among other things, loneliness. There were times, understandably, when she found it hard to come to me and open up. Instead, she found safety with her mother and, thankfully, that kept her from a sentence of utter isolation. (I'm so grateful for the teamwork Mary Jo and I enjoy; I explain this in more detail in Prologue: Invitation to Moms at the start of this book.)

Still, Ellie shared her story of the way she has been living because of her agreement with that message. She has been living this initiation journey far too alone. At times she has been hesitant to engage because of how I have been missing her heart. My heart sank. Her vulnerability was so good, so insightful. Her grieving has opened the door for healing to begin as she has allowed herself to feel the full weight of the wound. Her grieving was also a gift; it opened the door to healing, not just for her, but for me as well. Her vulnerability gave me the chance to be vulnerable myself as I owned it and asked her forgiveness. She graciously offered it.

Part of the ongoing healing for me has been in my own grieving as I continue bringing the weight of that moment before God. But it isn't in shame. I am a man. I am imperfect. My own story continues to unfold, and it was my own unhealed brokenness that spilled out and wounded my daughter. Of that I am guilty. But the story of my brokenness and wounding of my daughter is nowhere near the end of the story. (Just as it wasn't the end of the story for Ben.) God continues to father me right alongside my children. We are already moving into the freedom and shared healing Ellie's courageous vulnerability made possible. And again, this also happened with Ben. In both relationships, we forgive, learn, pick each other up, dust each other off, and keep going. My daughter's vulnerability opened the door to rescuing the full joy of this journey of initiation that the ungrieved and unhealed shame would have stolen.

So it is for you and your children. In having that kind of relationship with their earthly father, your kids will also learn that kind of relationship with their heavenly Father. They will learn to grieve things big and small: limitations, loss, failure, wounds, betrayal, abandonment, and more. Let them know that it is perfectly understandable and okay for them to feel what they feel in hard moments. Because, of course, they do! After all, who can truly trust a God from whom they have come to believe they have to hide their deepest hurts, fears, and doubts? The reality is, God already knows what we are truly feeling.

While we might think it is courageous and God-honoring to try to hide or pretend that the difficult feelings (even those difficult feelings toward God himself) aren't there, the reality is that anything other than complete authenticity and vulnerability with him in our grief is simply a version of self-deceit. It is not the kind of relationship you want with your children, nor God with his.

Ellie could have simply stuffed it all away in an attempt to ignore the hurt and pain. She didn't do that. Instead, she moved toward God's invitation to feel the full weight of the wounding and, with him, to grieve it all. The truth is, he cares deeply about all of it (1 Peter 5:7). Your kids need to know that you do too. Over the years I have missed my daughter's heart in her emotional life and hurt her with the message that she needed to be fixed. In that moment at the breakfast table, my daughter's courage gave me a chance to offer her what she had been needing: a strong shoulder to cry on, a warm hug, and permission to express it all. She had already started receiving that from her heavenly Father. She also needed that from her imperfect and very grateful earthly father. It is in moments like these, men, that you will build deep wells of trust between you and your children and, more importantly, deep wells of trust between your kids and God.

FORGIVENESS

AS I FATHER YOU . . .

At that point Peter got up the nerve to ask, "Master, how many times do I forgive a brother or sister who hurts me? Seven?" Jesus replied, "Seven! Hardly. Try seventy times seven" (Matthew 18:21, 22, The Message).

I've always loved Peter. There are many moments like this one between him and Jesus, times when Peter unwittingly presents a "teachable moment." Peter was a hardened fisherman, extremely familiar with the unforgiving demands of earning a living from the catch. It was a hard life lived in community with hard men. And Peter was a Hebrew. Peter would have known that the common teaching of the Pharisees at the time was that forgiveness was to be offered three times.[5] When he presented this question to Jesus, it's clear Peter already knows Jesus' heart for forgiveness is bigger than that. So he doubles what is the standard thought of the day and adds one for good measure! Imagine his surprise, then, when Jesus, with a slight chuckle, says, "Try seventy times seven." No, he didn't mean 490 times, and then that is it, the end. He meant that we are to never stop forgiving. Ever. Just as I imagine Peter and the disciples doing, on hearing these words we all sit in disbelief.

God's invitation to forgive is an invitation, a very strong one. Okay, well, it is more like a command. Still, forgiveness is something we resist strongly. This is one of those "invitations" that feels more like a stern taskmaster making us—no, demanding us—do something we really don't want to do and that we really don't feel like we should have to do. Yes, Jesus makes clear here that he is serious about this command. But his seriousness is not in contradiction to what we are learning to see as his true heart toward us. It is perfectly consistent. His seriousness is not about forcing us into mindless obedience. Instead, it is still very much about what he wants for us and, therefore, reveals just how critical the invitation is. Remember, his heart toward you is rooted in fierce passion for intimacy. Forgiveness, then, must be a vitally important issue for us to understand. Your life of intimate sonship depends on you understanding . . . and practicing . . . forgiveness. So, once again, we have extracting to do.

Forgiveness is extremely important but also very misunderstood. I taught for several years in an elementary school where I saw this confusion play out regularly. In my interactions with the kids, a big part of my job included teaching them conflict resolution. On those occasions when one child offended another, I would work to help them understand what they had done and how hurtful it was to their classmate. In other words, just as we discussed above, I would work to help them understand their guilt and take ownership. Once there, I would ask what they thought they should do next. Just about every time they would immediately recognize the need to apologize, which is where the confusion would come in. Once the offender apologized, the other child almost always said, "That's okay. I forgive you." In other words, forgiveness automatically means "that's okay." But that is not a necessary part of forgiveness. To be honest, this is a confusing issue for adults as well . . . and maybe even for you. So let's take this opportunity to build in a healthy understanding of forgiveness for ourselves so we can help our kids have a healthy understanding of the issue as well.

The reality is that, for many people, forgiveness is difficult because people feel so conflicted about it. It might seem fairly easy as kids. But as the years go on and the offenses we experience become more impactful, it becomes much more difficult to feel, about the offense, "That's okay." Yet Jesus teaches us to forgive throughout the Gospels. Why? Because the alternative is utter poison for our hearts. We cannot hold onto bitterness, anger, and hatred and also have room for intimacy, peace, healing, joy, and all the things God wants for us. So Jesus tells us to forgive, and he does it in a most sobering way.

"In prayer there is a connection between what God does and what you do. You can't get forgiveness from God, for instance, without also forgiving others. If you refuse to do your part, you cut yourself off from God's part" (Matthew 6:14, 15, The Message).

This means to let it go. To hand it off to him and trust that he knows best (much better than I possibly could) how to deal with the offense and the offender. It is a bold declaration that the cross is enough. But the letting go is extremely difficult if we don't untangle the confusion around the issue.

So let's talk about what forgiveness is not. It is not always easy. Sometimes it is a process, something that may very well need time, perseverance, and God himself to make happen. It is not having to pretend that everything was okay. Heck, it probably wasn't. It hurt. It was wrong. It cost you something, ruined something, or set in motion consequences that could very well be ongoing. No, it's not okay. (At the same time, a quick word: humility in this business of forgiveness is essential too. It is always possible that there is another side to the apparent offense that I'm not fully understanding and seeing.)

Forgiveness does *not* mean having to trust someone who has not proven trustworthy. Nor is it the same thing as reconciliation. *Forgiveness only depends on me.* Reconciliation depends on two people coming together in a healthy, restored relationship of trust and mutual respect. I cannot achieve reconciliation by myself. I can pursue it, but ultimately the other person has to want reconciliation as well. Forgiveness, though, isn't about the other person. And it's not really even about the offense. It is about me and my heart. When Jesus invites me to forgive, he is not saying I need to blindly and foolishly trust someone who is not trustworthy. He is not saying I have to continue to make myself vulnerable to continued offenses. Instead, he teaches us to forgive because he knows how important it is to guard our hearts. Bitterness, anger, and hatred are all-consuming if they go unchecked. They will rob us of intimacy with him and keep us from living out of the ultimate reality of our belovedness.

AS I FATHER YOU . . . SO YOU FATHER YOUR CHILDREN

So, much as we discussed in God's invitation to grieve, we cannot be trite about this issue of forgiveness. Forgiveness is not a command to be naive about, to foolishly "keep taking it on the chin" for Jesus. In other words, help your child understand that forgiveness is not about sacrificing their dignity or diminishing their self-worth. When properly understood, it is exactly the opposite. And this is exactly why Jesus is so adamant about it.

Still, forgiveness is hard, even when we have a much healthier understanding of it! When your kids are hurt and are trying to deal with real pain caused by someone, they need to know that everything they are feeling is okay and understandable. We have spent a lot of time looking at the story of Adam and Eve. We came to appreciate that there was an original design for our relationship with God. But there was also an original design for our relationship with each other. There are things we are made to want and need from one another. So when someone has hurt us or failed us, the anger, sadness, betrayal, or abandonment we feel is coming from something divine. Our misunderstanding of forgiveness, in part, lies in the belief that what we feel in those moments is shameful. It isn't. You want it made right. You want justice. Your kids do too. God knows that. He gave you and your kids that desire. Which is why this invitation to forgive is not a command to pretend otherwise. Instead, his invitation is to grieve the pain with him and then trust him with the work of making all things right. Forgiveness can never mean that we give up on our longing for healthy, respectful, honoring, and fulfilling relationships, especially with those closest to us. Our ongoing desire for those kinds of relationships is what moves us toward reconciliation—even if the other person does not. Regardless, the hope for reconciliation starts with forgiveness. Forgiveness is God's gracious invitation to grieve the hurt and, ultimately, lay it down so we can then make room for him to be for us everything we have needed but not received. In other words, forgiveness is yet another invitation to find and receive healing, healing that simply will not come any other way. This is how he's fathering you.

As he fathers you, so you father your children.

Next: It is the pattern of fatherhood. Our heavenly Father invites. We respond and move toward the invitation. The work of God in our heart always starts with an invitation. We've only explored a few. There are many more.

Chapter Nine

VISION

If people can't see what God is doing, they stumble all over them-
selves; But when they attend to what he reveals, they are most blessed
(Proverbs 29:18, The Message).

As I write the first part of this chapter, I can reflect and say this has been a delightful morning. We just celebrated a wonderful Thanksgiving break together with my dad's and brother's families. Then we came home and did something we had never done with our kids. We bundled up for a walk in a winter wonderland here in Michigan, heading out to a local farm to cut down our Christmas tree. We spent the rest of the day decorating the tree and our home together, soaking up the simple joy of the Christmas season. The whole weekend was like that, really: something straight from the heart of God as he invited us to delight in him and each other. It was all so very good.

But God's invitation to delight in him and *with* him isn't limited to holiday weekends. It is an ongoing, open invitation I am learning to look for and move toward. Admittedly, this is something I have been learning for some time and still have much to learn about. This morning, though, I didn't have to search long. In fact, it greeted me before I even got out of bed. When my alarm went off, I woke enough to realize that I really could use some extra sleep. I know: who doesn't feel that in the morning? Except this morning, I did have a little extra time and felt the invitation to sleep a little longer. So I did. Yes, I most certainly had some work to do. But it doesn't always mean there is no room to recognize and move toward invitations like that one. He is always inviting, and he had more for me. So before I rushed off to crack open my computer and get to work, he invited me to continue receiving his love and goodness. I got up, dressed, and filled my mug with hot coffee. Then I put on my coat, hat, and gloves and stepped out our back door to one of my favorite places to start a day. Outside, on our back deck, I was greeted with the cold, crisp winter air, the crunch of freshly fallen snow under my feet, and a horizon filled with a sunrise pushing away the crescent moon and the last remnant of the night. My heart sang "Good morning, God" as I breathed it all in. Then I came inside to a warm fire and the joy of our beautiful little tree. There I sat, praying, delighting, receiving . . . a silent yet life-giving presence with God. I was ready for my day.

In the last chapter, we explored God's good heart for us through his open invitations. The invitations he's had for me and my family over this Thanksgiving weekend, and again this morning, are more examples of what that has looked like for me these last few days. Of course, not all of his invitations are easy. But they are all good, very good.

It is the pattern of fatherhood. Our heavenly Father invites. We respond and move toward the invitation. As we are fathered, so we father our children. Your life of intimate sonship with God, then, is the strength and source of what you turn and offer to your children. The pattern always starts with an invitation. There are so many things he can't wait to share with his sons and daughters, and all of these invitations add up to something. He is freeing us from what is broken and dysfunctional and freeing us for wholeness and healing. In doing so, he is freeing us for a life he designed for us. Yes, it is a life he very much intends for us to see and understand for ourselves. In fact, it is another invitation: to catch a vision for the work he is doing as he fathers us and, as fathers ourselves, to help our kids understand and live into that vision as well. Our heavenly Father most certainly is up to something in the lives of his children. Paul wrote to the Philippians:

And I am certain that God, who began the good work within you, will continue his work until it is finally finished on the day when Christ Jesus returns (Philippians 1:6, NLT).

This is a bold and hopeful statement. But if you're at all like me, I can't help but wonder what the "good work" is. Fortunately, Paul gets a little more detailed with the Corinthians.

And we all, who with unveiled faces contemplate the Lord's glory, are being transformed into his image with ever-increasing glory, which comes from the Lord, who is the Spirit (2 Corinthians 3:18).

Okay, so his work is transforming us into Jesus' image or, as other translations say it, "Christlikeness." As God fathers us, then, drawing us deeper into our sacred identity and, at the same time, connecting us more fully to our sacred roles as fathers, he is working to free us, heal us, and transform us more and more into the likeness of Jesus. That is a really beautiful and enticing thought and yet, at the risk of sounding irreverent . . . also very unsatisfying.

I'm guessing I'm not alone in feeling that way. I know; we're not supposed to say things like that about Scripture. Don't get me wrong. I am grateful for the insight God had for us through Paul's words. I am highly intrigued by the idea that God is at work growing me into Christlikeness. I'm guessing you are too. But, really, am I alone in feeling like that statement begs a question? Aren't you right there with me, asking: What does that *mean*?

If that is a question you are struggling to answer, again I remind you: you are not alone. As it turns out, it was a question God awakened in me almost immediately in the aftermath of my crash and burn—in fact, right in the middle of it. I vividly remember sitting in on a discussion about discipleship. My wife and I had not yet moved on from the church where I had been serving, so I was trying to find ways to still make contributions. In this case, a few of us gathered to explore what discipleship might look like for our community. Our meeting didn't last long. We started with a simple question: "What is discipleship?" Having been through four years of seminary, I confidently raised my hand and offered the very theologically sound answer that you might expect: "growing in Christlikeness." As soon as I answered, though, I felt the weight of the next question. So did everyone else. For a moment, nobody wanted to ask aloud what we were all thinking. So I finally just said it: "And . . . what does that mean?" None of us could answer. I was personally bothered by that. I remember sitting there thinking about my education, and here was maybe one of the most important questions we could ask . . . and I had no answer. I learned many things over those four years in seminary. But in that moment I questioned everything about how valuable that education was. It seemed to me that something was fundamentally off that such a crucial question could have been missed so badly. It was unsettling—and yet also very motivating.

Something began to stir and, as it turned out, God was using that moment to extend an invitation to me. As I grew to embrace my new role as a full-time dad, so too did my desire to grow to understand God's work in our lives. I began to see that my question about Christlikeness and my sacred role as a father were very much connected. I had reawakened to my divine responsibility as a father, but I also felt the lingering frustration and fear of not really knowing what it meant to fulfill that responsibility, a responsibility that seemed far too important to be left to my "best guess." Yes, I had made the connection that my responsibility, in the broadest sense, was partnering with God in his work of transforming my children into Christlikeness. By now, though, that simply wasn't enough. It gave me great hope to realize that it wasn't enough for God either. The promise of this verse is so hopeful it's worth reading again:

> *If people can't see what God is doing, they stumble all over*
> *themselves; But when they attend to what he reveals,*
> *they are most blessed* (Proverbs 29:18, The Message).

This proverb became a part of my daily plea to God. "If people can't see what God is doing, they stumble all over themselves." The implication is clear. He doesn't want us stumbling all over ourselves! No, this proverb doesn't mean that we can master our understanding of God himself, that we can attain knowledge and understanding so complete that mystery and uncertainty are eliminated. To know and love God is to accept mystery and uncertainty. He is, all at once, beyond our capacity to fully understand and, at the same time, imminently close, intimate, and relatable. This proverb refers to what he has revealed. For that which he has revealed, then, he doesn't want us guessing and feeling around in the dark! He wants us to see what he's up to, understand it, and "attend to," or "live into," it. So, daily, my interaction with God became a heart cry to see clearly what his work is in transforming us into Christlikeness. I knew that to understand that would also be to more completely understand my divine responsibility as a father. God invited me to bring the question to him. And I did . . . for more than a year.

What I was unable to see at the time was the wisdom of how he was answering. He allowed the ongoing heart cry to fuel an eager and passionate search. My crash and burn had me ready to unlearn old assumptions and make room for new ideas and a deeper understanding of God's heart toward me, my identity in him, and what it looks like to love others well. It was a season of curiosity and exciting new discoveries as I read Scripture with a humility and openness I lacked before my crash. I prayed, studied, listened, asked questions . . . prayed, studied, listened . . . and read still more. All the while I clung to the promise that God did want me to see what he was up to, to attend to it, and, then offer that to my family.

Through it all he was also fathering me. Bit by bit, the beautiful mixing of my own eager searching and my growing understanding and experiences of intimate sonship were coming together. All the invitations were adding up to something. Then the moment when it all came together arrived, and a picture emerged, a vision for what he had been doing in my life. It took more than a year because my Intentional Dad is not and never has been interested in cold, relationless obedience. Nor is he interested in the lifeless hand-off of knowledge. His fierce passion for intimacy with me meant that he was going to answer my question by inviting me on a journey of discovery with him. He would instruct me, first and foremost, by teaching me sonship. I was learning to be fathered and, in the process, learning to father my children. Only then was I ready to receive the understanding I had been longing for.

He was starting with the end in mind: training, refining, teaching, loving, prompting, comforting, hardening my resolve, softening my pride and arrogance . . . always inviting and fathering me. He's doing the same with you. He is growing us up, freeing us from our small stories and shallow pursuits. It is work that makes the enemy tremble. If it hasn't become clear just yet, let me make it plain, beloved son. Your life of intimate sonship has a strength and weight to it that you are only beginning to understand. You were made to be a powerful force for good in this world . . . and to come alongside God on behalf of your kids to train and prepare them for the full weight of their lives as well.

What does it mean that God is working to transform his sons and daughters into "Christlikeness"? It means he is growing us up to live as

Jesus lived. There is a design for how God wants us to live. Jesus' thirty-three years on this earth demonstrated it. As fully adopted sons and daughters of God, then, we inherited this design. It is an inheritance I desperately wanted to understand as a beloved son and an intentional dad. After more than a year of seeking clarity, God opened my eyes to an awe-inspiring vision that painted a picture of the life Jesus lived—the same life our Intentional Dad designed for you and me. This vision became a framework that would guide how I parented my children.

You and I were made to live a life of intimate sonship with God. It is a life marked in these ways:

Guided By Wisdom

Uncompromising in Loyalty

Inspired By Freedom

Motivated By Oneness

Firm in Character

Driven By Love

This is the work he is doing in you. It is the work he is doing in your wife and kids. I know how my heart came alive as a father as I imagined my young children growing into adults living intimately with God—a life marked by Wisdom, Loyalty, Freedom, Oneness, Character, and Love. It was an extremely motivating realization, not just for the hope and awe inspired by "seeing what God is doing," but in seeing that, also understanding, more clearly than I ever had, my divine responsibility to my kids. There is so much to discover and understand with each of these works. It is more than I can fully explain in this book. Furthermore, to do so would rob you of an invitation, the same one God extended to me. This invitation is to join him on a journey of discovery for yourself and then to bring your kids alongside for their own journey. That journey of discovery has been an important part of each stage of my kids' initiation process. To get you started, I have included Scripture references in Appendix C for your own exploration of these ways God is growing us up. Beyond that, there are other next steps at the end of chapter ten for you to consider. So, this is not the place to go into an in-depth exploration and commentary. What I can do, though, is get practical and offer some experiences of what it has looked like for me and my family to be fathered into this life. A life we have been learning together, now for well over a decade.

GUIDED BY WISDOM

A life guided by wisdom is a life lived in the intimate counsel of God. It is a life marked by an attentiveness to his leading and a readiness and willingness to listen, even when his counsel isn't what we want or expect to hear.

I have described the aftermath of my crash and burn as wilderness. What I mean by that is, for the first time in my life, I found myself in a circumstance that left me with nothing that I could cling to as an external source of identity. No longer in ministry, I couldn't call myself a pastor. Having left behind a career at Ford, I could no longer call myself an engineer. And with no sense of what I would do now, I didn't even have a direction I could point to. I didn't know who I was. The wilderness wasn't just about identity, though. The wilderness was a stripping away of everything I might turn to other than God for my sense of well-being. For me, that also meant leaving behind my idol of church. Yes, church had become an idol for me. Church had become my great hope to prove my worthiness to God and the world. God's invitation into the wilderness meant leaving all that behind as well. The wilderness, then, was nothing but me standing naked before God. It was very unsettling. The last thing, then, that I wanted to hear (much less do) was God telling me to stay in it. So, of course, I began searching, and I did find something that felt promising, a new career in pastoral counseling. It seemed to check so many boxes and, best of all, would get me out of the wilderness. I really wanted to do it but . . .

My heart, by now, was crying out for healing. Not knowing who I was without something to provide a sense of identity was a huge warning sign, something I could no longer ignore. So I asked some friends to help me make sense of the internal conflict. I've already shared the story of the fateful evening that a friend stripped away all the confusion by simply pointing out that my way forward was to be a dad. It was the last thing I wanted to hear. It was also exactly what I *needed* to hear. Wisdom was calling and God was offering his counsel. I wanted a quick exit from the wilderness. Instead, he was inviting me deeper into that area of messiness. After that night, I knew I was at a crossroads.

Around that same time, I came across a series on wisdom given by Andy Stanley. It was a series based on his book *The Best Question Ever*. In that series he offered an incredibly practical question that, if we have the courage to ask it, has the profound impact of turning our hearts and minds to the intimate counsel of God:

"In light of your past experiences, current circumstances, and future hopes and dreams, what is the wise thing to do?"[1]

Though I didn't like what he said, a friend offered me the gift of clarity that night: ignore the warning signs and take the quick exit or go against all my instincts and move toward God's invitation instead. New career, new life, new mountains . . . or anonymity, daily wrestling matches with shame, and nowhere to hide. Andy Stanley's question captures exactly how God was fathering me in this moment. As much as I wanted to deny it, I knew my friend was right. I asked for help discerning God's counsel. Through my friend, his counsel was offered. What I was left with, then, was for me to respond. In light of my past experiences, current circumstances, and future hopes and dreams, what was the wise thing to do? It was clear. I chose to be guided by wisdom and move toward God's invitation.

My heart needed healing—badly. God had me right where I needed to be, and the work began. You know that part of the story. It was God's wisdom that guided me through that season, and I am so overwhelmingly grateful. With time I began to see that the wilderness was not a curse at all. It was where my initiation into intimate sonship would happen. It was where I found healing and started learning God's true heart toward me: I'm loved, I belong, and I have nothing to prove. Had I run from the wilderness, I would have chosen to run from God and my sacred role as a father to my children, and from all that would come in the subsequent years as we shared God's initiation journey as a family. I don't know how things would have gone had I ignored God's invitation. It is not hard to imagine, though, that my ignored and unhealed heart would have been a source of great pain to me, my wife, and my kids.

That, really, is maybe the most difficult part of this work. To be guided by wisdom . . . to listen for and heed God's counsel. Often, this leads to accepting him telling us what we need to hear, not what we want or expect to hear. Our heavenly Father does that as an outpouring of his good heart toward us. It is something we also must do in fathering our children: an outpouring of our good father's heart toward them. He's growing us up, and growing up means learning this principle to live daily in his intimate counsel: to be guided by wisdom.

UNCOMPROMISING IN LOYALTY

It's easy to love God when things are going well. But loyalty is tested in turmoil and conflict. Loyalty is authentic, raw honesty with God in the storms of life held in tension with a gritty resolve and commitment to God's goodness, trueness, faithfulness, and trustworthiness.

We don't like suffering. It feels silly saying it, kind of like saying water is wet. It's pretty obvious. Which is why it is so surprising to read passages like this in Scripture:

Friends, when life gets really difficult, don't jump to the conclusion that God isn't on the job. Instead, be glad that you are in the very thick of what Christ experienced. This is a spiritual refining process, with glory just around the corner (1 Peter 4:12, 13, The Message).

Other translations say things like "rejoice" or "be very glad." It is surprising and, frankly, confusing. Let's be real here: there is nothing about suffering that feels joyful. When the storms of life are raging, when it feels like we are on the front lines of an intense battle, I am not rejoicing! Neither are you. Those seasons can be extremely intense. And when we're in them, it can feel like there is no end and, worst of all, as though God has completely failed and abandoned us. What makes this so confusing, then, is being told to "be glad," as though we have to pretend everything is okay. So we do our best to put on a happy face and tell ourselves, and each other, cute little slogans like "everything happens for a reason" or "God is good, all the time." The one thing we can't do, of course, is allow how we're really feeling to be acknowledged or, worse, come out. That would be . . . disloyal.

This couldn't be more wrong.

Let me illustrate with a story of my oldest son's initiation journey. Specifically, it is the story of his last year in a decade-long process we had been living together. It was his senior year of high school, and we all had dreams of a very special year in his life, a kind of victory lap and year-long celebration of my little boy who had grown up. It was an emotional time for me as I reflected on almost eighteen years watching him grow. He was a highly accomplished wrestler and an even better student. More than that, my little boy had now stepped to the threshold of manhood, and I could see the fruit of our long initiation journey beginning to blossom. I was excited to see what God had in store for his final high school year.

We were particularly excited for his final season of wrestling. Wrestling was something he and I shared in, with me as his coach through most of his youth career. We had invested a lot of time and effort, father and son, as he worked to become one of the best wrestlers in the state. But injuries began catching up to him his junior year. It led to surgeries on both knees in the offseason. With the surgeries behind him, we were hopeful for a healthy senior year and one last season to celebrate everything coming together. However, it wouldn't take long for that dream to start looking more like a nightmare.

Things started happening. In a nutshell, he reinjured his knees and, of course, was unable to continue performing at an elite level. People he once thought he could rely on and trust seemed to turn on him. The betrayal ranged from simply dismissing the severity of his injuries to outright, vicious accusation and rejection. Every day the betrayal seemed to get worse. Every day I watched my son leave for school in physical, emotional, and spiritual pain knowing that he had to go back into the storm. Day after day this nightmare played out. It was heartbreaking, and there was very little I could do about it. It was one of the most difficult experiences I've had as a father. All I could do was put my arm around him every night and just be at his side—stand guard, as best I could, over his heart and see him through it all.

Imagine then, if, as his father, I had come to him in the middle of that nightmare and told him things like "everything happens for a reason." Or if I had dismissed his pain and suffering by reminding him just how good God is. It would have been a violent blow to his heart and a trampling of the pain and turmoil he was feeling, pain and turmoil that was sacred. Why? Because it would have brought a message of shame—that something was wrong with him for not "rejoicing" in the storm. It would have cut him off from intimacy with me and, far more importantly, with his heavenly Father. In other words, it would have undermined everything we had shared together on our initiation journey and the previous nine years I had spent pointing him to and training him for: a life of intimate sonship with God.

Though it was his storm, I felt the pain and turmoil along with him. Like him, I wondered aloud what God was doing. It seemed like God had abandoned my son and left him to face a bewildering barrage of hatred, rejection, betrayal, and abandonment. None of it made sense, and the vitriol directed at him had become incredibly intense. My son and I both felt the grief of him having to endure this nightmare instead of the triumphant celebration that should have been happening. I know how I would have felt if someone had told me to simply "be glad."

We didn't go there. My son was mad. He was hurt. He wondered, daily, what God was doing. Or if he even cared. I did too. And we simply didn't have the capacity to pretend otherwise. So we didn't. No slogans. No false pretenses. Just a daily offering of our rawest emotions and my son's incredible courage to go into the fray again the next day. He just kept showing up. It was an inspiring display of resolve.

There would be an end, though, and it was glorious. On the final day of the season, the team was wrestling for a state championship. My son, having received effective short-term treatment for his knees, had started wrestling closer to his elite level again. He was in the lineup and, as he took the mat for what would be the final match of his career, I was an emotional wreck. Yes, of course we wanted to see him wrestle well. But as his father I knew he'd already won. As he took the mat one last time, I watched a young man of incredible character, courage, resolve, honor, and grit step into the spotlight. He would go on to win his match, one of only three victories for his team that day. The referee raised his hand. It was a fitting metaphor for a much bigger story than an insignificant high school wrestling match. My son ran off the mat and straight into the stands where we embraced each other . . . and cried. Even now, I'm emotional remembering the moment. I held him tight and told him how proud I was, that he had endured so much and rose above it all. Later, another dad sought me out to tell me just how inspiring it was to watch my boy endure that season. He knew very little of everything that happened, but he saw what I saw: a man had emerged through it all. And it was glorious.

Ben and I both needed several weeks to decompress and recover from it all. With time, though, I began to understand the full significance of the experience. Something much bigger was happening through the storm. This was a "spiritual refining process." Yes, the painful experience of the season came from people he had once trusted. But, really, through those relationships, it was the enemy throwing everything he had at my son. Why? As I had a chance to start putting everything in the bigger context of the true story we live in, I began to see that the true enemy through it all was our mortal enemy, Satan himself. One thing I have learned through the years: our enemy reveals what he most fears. Often, it is revealed in the intensity of his warfare. I started to see that the vicious warfare he unleashed on my son was, really, a backhanded compliment. He feared what my son was becoming: a fully initiated man. (I have more to say about that in the next section.)

We were on the cusp of a decade of intentional fathering, and I had given everything I knew how to give my son. Our family had been following God into the unknown for more than a decade at that point, venturing into things none of us had ever experienced. I didn't recognize, then, God's finishing work. What I learned in that experience is that everything I had to give to my son, all the intentionality I offered, in the end, was never going to be enough. Why? Because the outcome of the journey was always, ultimately, leading to a final hand-off. God gave us our son. It was our job to usher him to adulthood, where we would give him back. As a child he wanted and needed to know from his parents that he was loved, that he belonged, and that he had nothing to prove. He also wanted and needed us to usher him into adulthood, training him and preparing him to live intimately with God and to receive that sense of sacred identity from God himself. That hand-off, ultimately, is a spiritual refining that happens without us parents. It was something I could not, nor should, do for my son. The threshold of initiation is crossed when, standing face to face with Jesus, the child knows he or she has come into adulthood, that they have experienced Jesus himself speaking deep into their hearts: "Welcome to adulthood." In other words, he is the One who initiates.

And that is what was really going on for my son. Jesus was finishing the work. For nine years our family ventured on this journey not really knowing where it would lead. In the storms of that final year, it felt like God had turned his back and left us with nothing but despair and heartbreak. Still, my son persevered—and we learned just how wrong we were.

In the 2005 movie adaptation of C.S. Lewis's story *The Lion, The Witch, and The Wardrobe*, there is a scene that captures what was happening for my son. Peter, having been in the middle of a dizzying adventure, was still trying to sort out just how "real" the land of Narnia was. It was a lot to come to terms with. The story began with four English children displaced by the horrors of Nazi bombings in World War II. Sent away to the safety of the countryside, away from their mother, and worried about their father fighting in the war, the children have already endured more than any child should. Still, they make the best of their surroundings and begin to explore and do what children do . . . play. The youngest, during a game of hide and seek, finds a wardrobe and soon learns that it is actually a gateway into the magical world of Narnia. Soon, all the siblings join their youngest sister through the portal of a wardrobe and find themselves swept up in an epic tale of good versus evil. They learn that, in Narnia, they are long-awaited kings and queens, and their arrival is the fulfillment of a prophecy. It is a prophecy that tells of the return of a creature, a lion, named Aslan, and his return means the end of the illegitimate reign of the evil White Witch. Eventually, the children meet Aslan after a harrowing and desperate escape from the secret police: wolves sent by the White Witch to capture and kill the humans and put an end to any threat they might pose.

In a pivotal moment in the story, while talking with Aslan, Peter hears the screams of his two younger sisters. He runs to the cries and, to his horror, finds them desperately clinging for life as they hang from the limbs of a tree just out of reach of the deadly wolves. Peter springs into action and draws his sword. The lead wolf turns his murderous intent on his new prey. A boy stands facing this ravenous wolf, trembling as he awkwardly holds his sword the only way he knows how: pointy end between him and the enemy. Aslan rushes on the scene with his best soldiers right behind him and quickly subdues one of the wolves. Those soldiers begin to draw their swords to strike down the threat facing Peter. But Aslan speaks.

"No! Stay your weapons. This is Peter's battle."

It is a remarkable scene as Aslan stands watching it all unfold and does . . . nothing. The wolf unleashes a barrage of messages aimed at Peter's identity. He's not just content to go for the kill. He's bent on crushing Peter's heart as well. Peter stands his ground. The wolf circles closer and closer, the threat growing more and more imminent. And then the beast . . . lunges. Tension hangs in the air as we are left to wonder if Peter made it through the ordeal. Then, movement. Peter pushes the slain enemy off him and sits up shocked and disoriented. It takes him a moment to make sense of the ordeal as his sisters rush to swarm him with an emotional embrace.

Then Aslan speaks: "Peter, clean your sword." Aslan has Peter kneel before him and, on the spot, knights him.

"Rise, Sir Peter Wolf's-Bane, Knight of Narnia."[2]

Aslan stood by and watched as Peter faced down mortal danger. He did nothing as the enemy launched himself, with deadly intent, at the boy. He watched as the boy fell to the ground with the wolf's bared teeth inches from landing a deadly vice grip. How could a good and powerful creature such as this stately lion do . . . nothing? The rest of the scene plays out and we learn why: it was an essential moment for Peter's initiation. Aslan could not and would not knight him until Peter learned for himself what Aslan already knew: that he had what it took to withstand the most fierce and imminent threats the enemy could unleash. Peter learned, in that moment, what was most true about himself; the terrifying ordeal was the only way he was going to learn it.

In the weeks following that nightmare of my son's wrestling season, I realized the exact same thing had happened for him. Yes, it felt like God had turned his back. The experience had both of us bewildered and hurt. But his "inaction" was not abandonment. It was tremendous love. He was allowing the previous nine years of training to come together in a way that Ben could discover that he had what it took to withstand the enemy's best shot. He was battered, bruised, and scarred. Through it all, he stood tall, arm raised. The enemy spent it all in a desperate effort to crush my son's heart and spirit. He tried to drive a wedge of mistrust between him and God. Ironically, it was the courage to be honest about the abandonment he was feeling that kept that from happening. The enemy had failed. In the end, Ben kept showing up, an uncompromising resolve in God's goodness, trueness, faithfulness, and trustworthiness. My son had become a man.

INSPIRED BY FREEDOM

It is for freedom that Christ has set us free. Stand firm,
then, and do not let yourselves be burdened again
by a yoke of slavery (Galatians 5:1).

Freedom is life outside the constraints of shame and fear. True freedom is the central truth that you are loved, you belong, and *you have nothing to prove.* God's freedom is freedom from the burden of having to earn love and belonging and having to prove your worth. It is freedom for a fearless life rooted in God's immovable, unperishable, inexhaustible love. It is also essential for any man who longs to fulfill the promise of fatherhood. Let me say that again. Freedom—truly understanding and embracing the implications of freedom—is essential to any man who longs to embrace and fulfill the promise of fatherhood. Which means the enemy is highly invested in winning agreements that compel us, unwittingly, to forfeit our freedom. That also means that, to break the agreements, we will face some rather challenging invitations ahead, an "undoing" of some core beliefs you may not even be aware you have. God speaks to you: "Courage, beloved son." The time has come to be inspired by freedom and face, head on, some core beliefs that go to the heart of your divine responsibility and sacred role.

In my early days in the wilderness, this "undoing" was a huge and absolutely necessary part of how God was fathering me into a life of intimate sonship and, at the same time, reshaping and preparing me for the fatherhood journey in front of me. The painful experiences of my life in ministry and the culmination of my life with God to that point had me in a place that I was more than ready to question and unlearn old assumptions and relearn what God had for me in the wilderness. What I learned had a profound impact on my understanding of my divine responsibility to my kids. God completely reshaped fundamental core beliefs about myself, my calling of fatherhood, and my children. Which is why it is so important for me to share what I've learned. Believe me, I know how difficult it is to reexamine core beliefs. Some of you, understandably, will feel like this is an attack. Well, much of what we are about to discuss is a bit of an attack—but it is not my heart to attack you or anyone else. Instead, I am confronting what I believe to be enemy strongholds. If there is an attack, it is an attack on his work and his lies. The reality is that way too many men are being robbed of God and their calling by things they think are holy, sacred, and godly. With that background in place, let me start by going back into my story.

The story of my undoing started with the crash and burn that landed me in the wilderness. I've already shared how my immediate instinct was to look for a quick exit. I wanted out but, thankfully, didn't take the quick exit. My path forward was deeper into the wilderness. Which is where I would begin to understand, for the first time in my life, God's true heart toward me and, therefore, my true and sacred identity in him.

This is the part of my story that starts to make some uncomfortable. I had to be removed from the church life I had poured myself into to find a life of intimate sonship with God. With time I began to see that things I thought were essential and sacred had actually been massive barriers robbing me of the life and freedom I was beginning to experience. What was exposed in the wilderness was an idol I had given my heart to serving. We have already talked about the threat of religion to our lives of intimate sonship. It may be a shock to some to hear that Christianity, for many people, is a life of religion. God was opening the eyes of my heart in the wilderness. I began to see that before my crash and burn, my religion was Christianity. And the idol I truly gave myself to was what we might call "churchianity." God had ushered me to the wilderness and, once there, the undoing began through a steady dismantling of old agreements while finding more and more freedom each step of the way. He was fathering me, and I was learning to father my children. Let me go still deeper to share what I have learned through the years.

First, let's address an objection that could be lingering. No, I am not anti-church. I am anti-"churchianity." There is a big difference. Christ loves the church. He calls the church his bride, and our life of intimacy with him means that we are fully adopted into his family. There was an original design for our relationship with God. There was also an original design for our relationships with each other. Church, then, at its core is community shared by people who are learning to love one another well as we are also learning to love and be loved by God, living through his original design for us. So I love the hope and promise of church. I crave community like that. So do you. Yet precious few experience it. Why? That is an extremely important question. The answer starts to become clear in the side-by-side contrast of church versus "churchianity."

- Church started as a movement of ordinary people who had awakened to God's true heart toward them, his invitation to come home, and their sacred identities as his beloved sons and daughters. It was a movement that spread rapidly, in spite of severe persecution and oppression, around the message that you are loved, you belong, and you have nothing to prove.

- "Churchianity" is preoccupied with orthodoxy (right belief) and orthopraxy (right practice). It is a preoccupation rooted in the same illusion Jesus exposed in the story of the prodigal son: that God is primarily concerned with cold, relationless obedience. He is not.

- Church is a community of people alive to the reality of living in an epic story of good versus evil and a universe at war. It is a community of people fully engaged in their place in that story.

- "Churchianity" is an institution that is its own end. Service and devotion to the institution is the highest ideal.

- Church is an organic network of people led by the Spirit and marked by love and trust—trust in God and trustworthiness with each other.

- "Churchianity" is an organization designed to control, and the desire to control is rooted in fear: fear of each other and the wrath of an angry god.

- Church encourages the celebration of what is good, praiseworthy, noble, and right in God, each other, and ourselves.

- "Churchianity" is mired in what is wrong, broken, and far from God—especially as observed in others.

- Church is *unifying*, a community built on what unites us as human beings and our need for God.

- "Churchianity" is tribal; it is highly concerned with defining and distinguishing the parameters of belonging and winning converts to the tribe.

- Church is a community of people living in deep intimacy with God.

- "Churchianity" is a community led by select, trained professional clergy tasked with the job of communicating with God on behalf of a lost and needy flock largely perceived to be—maybe even encouraged to be—helpless consumers.

- Church equips, encourages, and inspires people to be powerful forces for good.

- "Churchianity" cripples people with the burden of trying ever harder to not be bad.

- Church is countercultural.

- "Churchianity," particularly in the United States, mirrors the host culture as it defines itself along political and ideological lines (i.e., progressive Christianity versus evangelical Christianity).

- Church operates primarily on the construct of family sharing in the struggles and celebrations of transformation.

- "Churchianity" operates primarily on the principles of a business, measuring success by bottom line metrics like attendance, number of conversions, buildings, and cash.

Ouch!

And Hallelujah. This is an invitation to freedom, to life outside the constraints of shame and fear. All religion is rooted in shame and fear, a fundamental pursuit of satisfying a god we have come to believe is primarily concerned with our behavior. "Churchianity" is the idol that the Christian religion compels us to worship, an idol built on messages. Look closely, beloved son. It would be easy to dismiss the invitation. But ask yourself: what is the story that animates your church experience? Is it a story about growing an organization, or is it a story of growing an organic movement? Is your experience of church more defined by what it wants from you or what it wants for you? Is your church experience more about compliance, or is it characterized by a community engaged and sharing in combat with an enemy bent on stealing, killing, and destroying our relationship with God and each other? What is more important? Loving God . . . really loving him? Or is it clearly more important that you attend, serve, and give? Is the community more concerned with your behavior or your story, your heart, and your need for healing?

What I would finally begin to see and understand in the wilderness was just how oppressive the spirit of religion was and how, unwittingly, I had been participating in that oppression. In his letter to the Galatians, Paul addresses this issue of religion and his conclusion is a bombshell. He equates the law—and by extension, any form of religion—with slavery (5:1). Any Hebrew reading those words would have been shocked to hear such an irreverent diagnosis. It may shock you to hear someone suggest that, for most, the experience of church, far too often, is no less oppressive. But that is the invitation: to break the agreements that have held you under the oppressive thumb of religion. It is breaking the agreement with the premise of fear that is behind all religion and the foundation on which the idol of "churchianity" rests. It is breaking the agreement of loyalty and devotion that "churchianity" demands. Yes, we are taught by Jesus to love the church, but this means loving the people! Your love, devotion, and loyalty is not to an organization, institution, or select professional clergy operating from a premise of fear and a corrupted perception of God. Your devotion and loyalty is to God.

It is telling, isn't it, that Jesus lived a life filled with conflict? His conflict was almost always with the professional clergy of the day and the oppression of religion they thrust upon the people. He was a man these leaders could not contain and control. He was an affront to their sense of entitlement and a threat because he did not operate within the confines of their traditions. It was simply unthinkable that this man claiming to be God would associate with the ordinary rabble they dismissed as an offense to God. They scoffed at the recklessness of this Rabbi from Nazareth, one who had the audacity to invite fisherman, prostitutes, merchants, and tax collectors to be his disciples. He did and, at the same time, exposed their empty hypocrisy. So they plotted his arrest and murder.

Are we so foolish and naive to believe that the same arrogance and pride isn't part of that same religious spirit today? I invite you to break another agreement. The concept of calling is not limited to a career in vocational ministry, as though work in the kingdom of God is meant only for a select group of "favored children." Please don't misunderstand: the men and women who give their lives to shepherding, leading, and teaching others through ministry do extremely important work. And the vast majority of those men and women are humbly and sacrificially offering as best they know to give out of genuine love for their communities. I am not, in any way, wanting to diminish these beautiful brothers and sisters. What I can say, though, is the damage that the spirit of religion does to them and to those they lead and shepherd is real. The spirit of religion isolates pastors as "the flock" puts them on a pedestal. And it imprisons the "uncalled" in a state of perpetual dependence. It is a perverted and twisted ploy of the enemy, one cleverly delivered under the guise of godliness. It is a wicked lie.

The simple truth is, as sons and daughters of the king of the universe, each of us is called, and all have an irreplaceable part to play in this epic story in which we live. I simply point you to the calling that is the subject of this entire book: your calling to fatherhood. It is the most important calling any man with children has. It is sacred and is a role and responsibility with your children that nobody can replace. Your calling is not to build and serve a church. Your calling is to build and serve people, starting with you and your family and then the people in every sphere of your life. In building and serving your family, you are building and serving the church. In loving and serving the people in your life, you are building and serving the church and thus the wider kingdom of God. The church is not an organization. It is not a building. It is the *people*. And your calling starts with the children given you by God.

Jesus' freedom is available to all. Not by offering an alternative "rule-keeping" system but, instead, by offering this radical cosmos-altering idea that we are loved: deeply, intimately, completely. That we belong, and we have nothing to prove. This love not only cannot be earned, it cannot be lost. We are loved with all of our brokenness, ugliness, shame, and failure. This is why Paul says "neither our most conscientious religion nor disregard of religion amounts to anything" (Galatians 5:4-6, The Message). Why does he say this? Because it really doesn't amount to anything! There are no rules for God to love any of us. The only question in front of us, the one thing that matters, is whether we really are learning to believe it, receive it, trust it, and live out of it.

I acknowledge that this freedom issue can seem awfully scary. After all, it could start to seem that "anything goes." It is maybe the most common objection, that this kind of freedom is dangerous. Well, yes. Yes it is. But why should that stop us? We live in the context of a universe at war. We have an enemy that hates everything about us and about God's creation. Danger is an inescapable part of our reality. We can respond to that reality by agreeing with the messages of shame and fear that compel us to make agreements with religion in exchange for safety. But at what cost? You were made to be free. You were made to live outside the constraints of fear and shame. The agreements have cost you that freedom. And the agreements will cost the experience of that freedom for your family as well.

Freedom is not the same as "anything goes." Freedom is not just what you're freed *from*, it is simultaneously what you're freed *for*. Freedom is not, as Westerners want to define it, getting to do "whatever I want to do." Jesus' teachings all reinforced a much different definition: freedom is living life more and more fully according to the original design. There is an original design for our relationship with God and each other. Freedom is found in learning to live that design through a life of apprenticeship with Jesus, and it is rooted in the foundational principle of freedom: you are loved, you belong, and you have nothing to prove. It is not a license for less responsibility. It is a call both to more responsibility and yet another inspiring vote of confidence from God that we are up to increased responsibility, that we are empowered by the intimate life we are learning to live with him. In fact, it's more than that. His sons and daughters are not destined to be shielded and protected from the big, bad world. Quite the opposite. We are destined to rock the world for good. It is the enemy who shudders in the face of a fully initiated man or woman of God, not the other way around. Yes, we need grounding. We need understanding. We need guideposts and anchors. Thus the recognition that we have much to be responsible for.

"Churchianity" equates responsibility with compliance and submission to the authority of select professional clergy and compliance with an institution. That assumes, though, that people are not capable of truly knowing God for themselves and, thus, not able to distinguish his truth from lies. But if we are on a journey to initiating our kids, aren't we initiating men and women who are not only capable of the responsibility that comes with that freedom but also able to thrive in it? Doesn't it stir your father's heart to envision your kids as adults, at work, at play, with neighbors, friends, coworkers, and family, through all the highs and lows, and in the ordinary in between, freely moving in and out of circumstances and interactions? To envision them discerning God's presence and invitations, extracting the precious from the worthless, finding and offering healing, knowing the joy of a vibrant life with God and, in their freedom, freeing others to do the same? It is an inspiring picture of the kind of people and kind of life you are preparing your kids to live as fully trained and prepared adults. It is, in fact, a picture for all of God's sons and daughters. Kingdom work certainly includes many things local churches big and small offer. But the work those churches do is only a part of the much bigger scope of kingdom work that encompasses the entire community of God's family. John Mark Comer, author and founding pastor of Bridgetown Church in Portland, Oregon, says:

Church must become a thick web of interdependent relationships between resilient disciples of Jesus deeply loyal to the Way.[3]

That is church. That is freedom. That is what we all long for.

So if we start with the story of God through Scripture, we learn of his character, nature, and ways. We come to know him, intimately, and we come to understand ourselves ever more clearly. We also discover the beautiful truth that as beloved sons and daughters of Christ we have the indescribable gift of his very life in us. That, more than anything else, makes freedom so much less scary. The Spirit is wild and free and will come and go from and to the most surprising places (John 3:8). Part of the freedom God is cultivating in us is an ever greater capacity to follow his "wild Spirit" wherever it goes. These are really big ideas for us adults, let alone our children. Part of what we want to offer our kids is the inspiration of an initiation that includes a love for and deep respect for the kind of freedom (and responsibility that comes with it) that Jesus offers us. Maybe, just maybe, our kids won't have to "unlearn" quite as much as we might have to "unlearn" to make room for experiencing true freedom.

MOTIVATED BY ONENESS

Oneness is the characterization of a healthy relationship with God: the original design for our connection to him. Oneness is what motivates him and what he is fiercely passionate about. Oneness with us is what he wants us to be motivated by as well. It is an invitation to reject all other burdensome motivations rooted in fear and shame.

Freedom is anchored in a deeply rooted life of intimacy with God. Everything we have discussed in this book started with God's invitation to you for initiation into intimate sonship with him. Your initiation has been an awakening to and receiving of the ultimate reality of God's true heart toward you: you are loved, you belong, and you have nothing to prove. It is a love that is eternally secure (Romans 8). Your Intentional Dad is fathering you, and as he fathers you, so now you are learning to father your children. He has invited you into an intimate partnership to teach, prepare, and train your children for adulthood, to receive that same sense of sacred identity and intimacy from God as you are learning. However, while God's love toward us is unshakable, imperishable, and immovable, intimacy is anything but. It is why, the night before his arrest, Jesus prayed:

"I'm praying not only for them but also for those who will believe in me because of them and their witness about me. The goal is for all of them to become one heart and mind—just as you, Father, are in me and I in you, so they might be one heart and mind with us. Then the world might believe that you, in fact, sent me. The same glory you gave me, I gave them, so they'll be as unified and together as we are—I in them and you in me. Then they'll be mature in this oneness, and give the godless world evidence that you've sent me and loved them in the same way you've loved me"
(John 17:20-23, The Message).

Notice what he is asking the father to secure: unity.
Oneness.
We have been using the word intimacy. However, Jesus' prayer here calls out something even deeper. Oneness is the goal, and Jesus is praying for it because, in the reality of a cosmos at war, it is not an unshakable certainty. God's heart for us is characterized by a fierce passion for intimacy. More than that: oneness. And this is where we

have a part to play. Oneness is something we must fight for. I love how Dallas Willard says it:

Grace is not opposed to effort, it is opposed to earning.[4]

I had always appreciated and known the value of "spiritual disciplines." As I have shared this idea of oneness with my children, I have introduced them to the idea of disciplines as well. I know the word itself can evoke some very negative feelings, and some of that is deserved. However, in its simplest sense, a discipline is simply something you exercise for a benefit. So we engage in spiritual disciplines for a spiritual benefit. Or, perhaps instead of discipline, you talk about your routine or your rhythm. But regardless of the language you use, there is a trap we need to expose. Unfortunately, this issue of discipline can easily slip into just another expression of religion. I'm guessing that nagging feeling of shame is also something you are familiar with when it comes to journaling, praying, reading your Bible, and other acts of spiritual discipline. Honestly, what is the most predominant feeling that arises when you think of those things? Isn't it something along the lines of, *I ought to be doing more of that*? Or, on the other extreme, perhaps you feel a little bit of pride because you have gotten really good at "sticking with the program." Either extreme misses the point. These extremes are both symptoms of a transactional mindset built on a motivation of shame. Inevitably, it leads to the development of a rigorous program that promises to satisfy my duty to God. When shame is the motivation, "disciplines" become little more than a way to outrun the contempt of an impatient and demanding god . . . for a time. If we are going to keep the shame at a safe distance, it's a race we must run every day. It's a race we can never win, and it's exhausting. Here again, though, the invitation of freedom offers hope as we're learning the far-reaching implications of God's true heart toward us. Yes, we have a responsibility for the condition of our relationship with God. It is not because of an impatient and demanding god, though. Instead, it is a recognition of the reality of an enemy who is constantly on the prowl looking for opportunities to strike at your heart with his lies. He is always working to obtain the agreements that drive a wedge between us and the open arms of our heavenly Father to whom we belong.

Our enemy does not stop waging this assault. If we are truly to understand this initiation we are seeking for our children, we absolutely have to help them understand the true nature of the larger story we ourselves are in. All that is good, holy, pure, and right is opposed. Fiercely. Cruelly. Constantly. Yes, Jesus did satisfy the curse. And that did change everything. But the work is not done. It most certainly will be done some day but, in the meantime, we must be grounded in reality. We have an enemy who is absolutely committed to getting us to agree with one or both of his lies. My union with God is something *I have to fight for*—but it is a fight I can win because of the victory Jesus has already secured on our behalf. It is a daily battle to do two things:

- Cultivate a sense of awe about and delight in God's goodness, faithfulness, trueness, trustworthiness, majesty, wisdom—all his qualities;

- Reclaim my belovedness.

It is a fight motivated by a passionate desire for oneness, a longing to run into the loving embrace of our Abba, One who is always sprinting toward us, and a battle to reclaim who we are and to whom we belong. The motivation of shame, on the other hand, compels me to outrun a god I have come to believe is constantly evaluating my worthiness through cold, relationless obedience. It is a cruel perversion.

Let's head back to the idea of disciplines. There is a rich tradition of practices we can teach our children that are powerful and effective in this fight. There are also many wise authors we can learn from. The life-tested experiences and hard-earned wisdom is something I have been blessed by and, in turn, have encouraged my kids to practice. I encourage you to do the same. Here is a great starting list of resources.

Emotionally Healthy Spirituality by Peter Scazzero

Spiritual Direction by Henri Nouwen

Free by Kevin Butcher

Get Your Life Back by John Eldredge

The Ruthless Elimination of Hurry by John Mark Comer

There are many more. I happen to be a fan of journaling. Reading Scripture is an essential part of nurturing our understanding of God and our life with him. Prayer is our ongoing connection to the Trinity, and we absolutely want to encourage our kids to practice it and grow in their understanding of it. There are time-tested practices that apprentices of Jesus are wise to emulate, practices central to a life of apprenticeship with Jesus. Solitude, simplicity, Sabbath rest, participating in community, worshiping through music, reading, writing—all of this is good and extremely important. One thing the authors above have in common, though, is that everything they offer is built on an understanding that the motivation behind all they teach and share is oneness. More important than *what* we do is *why* we do it. Our prize . . . the reason . . . the motivation . . . is God himself. Eldredge writes, "We are talking about finding more of God. I assure you nothing, absolutely nothing, will bring you more of him than loving him."[5]

Is your motivation shame, shame rooted in a perception of a god demanding your cold, relationless obedience? It is a lie and it has tormented you long enough. Shame compels us to focus on what we do, prioritizing the things we assume promise to appease "god" the most. Oneness, on the other hand, compels us to focus on *who* . . . who we're fighting against and, far more importantly, who we're fighting to be with. The emphasis, then, cannot be on the things we do nearly as much as on why we do them. Which is yet another opening to be inspired by freedom. You may be familiar with the disciplines I have mentioned. But there are more: a hike through a forest can be a powerful way to cultivate awe as you awaken to God's intimate presence with you and the beauty of his work. So can kayaking, cycling, and golfing. Reading, cooking, and working can all be effective avenues for reclaiming my belovedness as I'm present to the moment with God in the midst of it, sharing in the joy, delight, and life we were made to have together. The more we learn to live from our birthright, in our sacred identities as beloved sons and daughters, the more we learn to love God for the treasure he is and the treasure we are to him. My motivation is for more of him, something I can experience the more I learn to look for him in the small and ordinary moments of day-to-day life. Yes, I have a responsibility, but responsibility can easily become synonymous with duty, with that cold, relationless obedience we have talked about. Oneness, however, is an invitation to shatter my compartmentalized boxes and begin learning to experience God in all I do. He is our prize. Oneness, not duty, is his design.

There is one more bit of wisdom we must understand and help our kids grasp recognition of as well. We live in an age of instant gratification. So it is important to balance everything with the countercultural idea that the expectation of grand "experiences" is not the prize—God is. Our fight for oneness is not about being entertained. Frankly, it is an idol that may be one of the biggest threats to oneness, not to mention the process of initiation. Initiation is the antithesis of instant gratification, a journey that will take years for you and your family. In addition, some of the things we practice could very well feel a bit tedious and difficult at times. For example, reading the Bible can be difficult. Let's face it, there are parts of Scripture that can be hard to understand and even more difficult to relate to. Some benefits of oneness that come from Scripture can take years to realize. Now, some benefits can and do come immediately as well. But it is not always going to be this radical, over-the-top, instantly gratifying experience. But even if it comes more slowly than we'd like, it doesn't mean it isn't valuable. So when we are talking about motivation, we are not advocating an irresponsible, fleeting, "the-moment-and-experience-is-king" kind of approach. Such an approach makes an idol out of a "spiritual high" where the value and health of our relationship with God is dictated by fleeting feelings and experiences. It's not too different from an adrenaline junkie always upping the stakes to achieve the emotional high. But what happens when, inevitably, the experience we are seeking isn't there? Or what happens when we are met with some of God's harder invitations? Our enemy eagerly awaits such an opportunity to swarm us, once again, with the illusion. Our motivation to fight for oneness is not just a sanctified way of justifying the pursuit of emotional highs or being entertained by God. Instead, we are claiming freedom, exercising wisdom, and moving toward God's invitations as he grows us to maturity. More often than not, that is found in the simple and ordinary moments of everyday life.

What's left, then, is to begin exploring the wide-open possibilities for you and your kids to pursue oneness. Try things. Practice things. Talk about things. Begin building an understanding now that our motivation is oneness, and that the reason we do something is far more important than what we do. Begin to build wisdom in understanding that some things we do may not seem to be very helpful today but, with time, do have tremendous benefit. Begin building wisdom with your children about the goodness of some of God's more difficult invitations. In targeting your heart, the enemy is seeking to rob you of intimacy, the oneness with God you were designed for. Which means we have to fight for it, guard it, and teach our kids to do the same. It is an essential part of the life God designed for us. So engage the fight for oneness with them and share the joy of the journey as you watch your kids grow into initiated adults who know what they are fighting for and how to battle for it.

Let me finish this section by sharing a story regarding my youngest son that, I think, captures the beautiful simplicity of fighting for oneness. Ian is now twelve years old. His initiation journey officially began the day after Ben's was completed. The journey begins, for us, with a baptism ceremony that is also the official launch of initiation. As part of Ian's preparation for that day, we explored this idea of oneness.

I explained to him that he was made to live in oneness with God, and that includes learning to hear from God. When introducing someone to the practice of hearing from God, I always start with the one thing we know our enemy will never utter with the authenticity, tenderness, delight, compassion and, even, playfulness that can only come from the Father's true heart: "I love you." So I invited my son, who was nine at the time, to give it a try. I asked him to get a notebook and pencil and head to our back deck to be alone with God. I invited him to simply sit with God and ask him to speak, specifically. To hear from God, "I love you."

Eagerly, he found a pencil and notebook and went outside. It was about ten minutes before he came back inside. I asked if he'd heard from God. Matter-of-factly, he said, "Oh yeah!" I asked, "Well, what did you hear?" "Here, I wrote it down," he said. He handed me his journal. There it was:

> Me: *"God, thank you for loving me."*
> God: *"You're welcome!"*

Beautiful.

FIRM IN CHARACTER

Then God said, "Let us make mankind in our image, in our likeness, so that they may rule over the fish in the sea and the birds in the sky, over the livestock and all the wild animals, and over all the creatures that move along the ground." So God created mankind in his own image, in the image of God he created them; male and female he created them (Genesis 1:26, 27).

Character is our reflection on the world. We are designed as image-bearers, reflections of God's integrity, goodness, trueness, justice, patience, kindness, and intentionality (just to name a few) back to his creation and the world around us. Soft character is that reflection perverted and twisted: the fruit of the enemy's lies reinforced by the illusion. Firm character is the fruit of healing that comes from God's intimate counsel and oneness with him. It is the result of moving toward and submitting to his invitations. Firm character grows out of God's heart toward us and, therefore, is something we are meant to receive, not achieve. It is something he wants for us, not from us.

I've already shared the story of my oldest son when he was 12, and the beautiful moment when he courageously told me just how much I had been hurting him. It was this work, character, that I had unwittingly turned into a cruel weapon of religion. Why? Well, I still had a lot to learn. I needed a lot more healing for my compulsion to climb mountains. (And still do.) Early in our initiation journey, I seized on this work of character because it readily meshed with a desire we dads share. It is the desire we have to raise our kids to be people of character. We envision our kids growing to be adults who are honest, hardworking, wise, successful, respectful, trustworthy, capable, and self-reliant. Like many dads, I had a mental list of my own and, without realizing it, equated that "character list" with my fatherhood scorecard. It was my new mountain to climb, and it was brutally unfair to my son. That was not my intent, of course. Still, in my brokenness, I turned something beautifully revealed by God into a crushing burden of religion. My root desire, though, was good. I'm a father. Of course I want my children to grow up to be people of character. It's a direct reflection of our heavenly Father. He wants all of his children to be people of firm character. It is a theme throughout Scripture. One well-known passage comes from Paul in his letter to the Galatians.

But what happens when we live God's way? He brings gifts into our lives, much the same way that fruit appears in an orchard—things like affection for others, exuberance about life, serenity. We develop a willingness to stick with things, a sense of compassion in the

*heart, and a conviction that a basic holiness
permeates things and people. We find ourselves involved
in loyal commitments, not needing to force our way in life,
able to marshal and direct our energies wisely.*

*Legalism is helpless in bringing this about; it only gets in the way.
Among those who belong to Christ, everything connected with
getting our own way and mindlessly responding to what everyone
else calls necessities is killed off for good—crucified*
(Galatians 5:22-24, The Message).

Man, that's a good list. Affection for others. Exuberance for life. Willingness to stick with things—just to name a few. I want to be a man of character. I want my kids to be people of character. The work our Intentional Dad is doing in crafting Christlikeness includes growing the fruit of firm character.

While my desire as a father for my kids to be people of character was good, there was, at the same time, something essential I was missing. Look again at what Paul has to say. He starts with a question: "What happens when we live God's way?" Then he answers: "He brings . . . " Those two words are what I was missing. *He* brings the gifts, *he* grows the fruit of firm character. In fact, that is a fundamental truth of all facets of his work in us.

Several years ago I heard an analogy offered by Tim Mackie, co-founder of the Bible Project, that I found immensely helpful. He observed a profound truth in his efforts to tend and care for a garden for the first time. In doing so, he noticed that his work involved caring for the soil, pulling weeds, keeping critters out, watering what was growing, and more. Yet he observed that, for all his work, he was completely helpless when it came to the actual growth of the plants and produce he'd hoped his garden would yield. *God is the one* who makes the fruit and vegetables grow. But this doesn't mean we have no part to play. A completely unattended garden will not yield anything desirable—only weeds. A poorly tended garden will yield some fruit, but sparingly. A well-tended garden, though, will produce abundantly. Our part is that of a gardener. Our motivation is oneness.

The same principle applies for this work of firm character. We tend the soil of our hearts to foster the conditions for growth. The good soil, then, is the fertile ground in which God brings forth fruit. It always starts with an invitation. Our heavenly Father is fiercely passionate about intimacy, about oneness with his sons and daughters. Every time we recognize and move toward his invitations, we are moving deeper into the oneness we were made for. We learn to live more and more deeply out of our belovedness by fighting for, by being motivated by, oneness with the Trinity. So just as I have no power to make a tomato grow in my garden, I have no power to make character grow in my heart. Instead, I can participate by doing all the things I know create the best conditions for growth. I recognize and move toward his invitations, and God takes it from there. Patience doesn't grow because I strive to be patient. It grows when I recognize the invitation within the irritation I'm feeling. I recognize it, move toward it, and, motivated by oneness, water the seed of patience by turning and surrendering to him in the moment. Turning and surrendering is our part as gardeners. I choose God's way. The result, Paul says, is growth. In this case, the fruit of patience. It is the same for any fruit: trustworthiness, integrity, gentleness, kindness, compassion, perseverance. All of it starts with an invitation from our heavenly Father, whose true heart we are learning to recognize. Yes, we want our sons and daughters to want the fruit of character, but from the start we also want them to understand what their part is in that growth process and what God's part is.

This issue of character is a central part of our responsibility as parents. I'm not saying anything you aren't already aware of—so aware that you are stepping into a years-long commitment to initiate your sons and daughters! You are quite aware of your responsibilities and, clearly, determined to rise to the challenge. Inevitably, you will encounter soft character with your kids. Those will be more difficult "truth-telling" moments. I know how difficult those can be. You want to help your son or daughter learn and grow, but there are tons of barriers that can make that task feel nearly impossible at times. So let me offer, from my experience, a few thoughts on some of my most-used spiritual "gardening tools" through the years.

1) The first tool comes back to the heart of a Father committed to the process of initiation. It is a **reminder that we start with the end in mind**. That's what this chapter (and, for those who want more, the Scripture references in Appendix C) is about: painting a picture—an understandable and livable picture—of what God is up to in each of us. You are guiding your son or daughter and building into them the skills to live into this life. It is a journey. I have always found it helpful in some of my more frustrating moments to remember that we are on a long journey to adulthood. Things may take longer than you'd like sometimes and, at other times, your kids will get things right away. So draw strength and patience from remembering that this is a long haul, and that you have clarity and direction, just as God promised he'd give. Trust it and, far more importantly, trust him.

2) The second tool, especially as it relates to these truth-telling moments, is one I mentioned before: **fierce rejection of shame.** Fight hard for this one. Speak to it often. Start some of these harder discussions with a reminder (to yourself and your son or daughter) that you refuse, absolutely refuse, to deal in shame. Fight hard to keep any messages of shame from entering the discussion. Simply do not allow the idea that something is wrong with your child to be part of what you talk about. Guilt? Sure, we absolutely have to talk about things for which they are guilty. Growth comes from them owning it, understanding it, and wanting to learn from it.

3) The third tool is related. **Belovedness**. Don't only fiercely reject shame, fiercely *champion* belovedness. This is the lifeblood of growth. It is what gives us the capacity and courage to own our guilt and stand before God. When you boil down the mission of truth-telling, that is it, isn't it? The work you do in initiating your children includes constantly pointing them back to their belovedness. And these truth-telling moments are actually the times when it can become the most relevant and real to them.

4) The fourth tool is one we discussed in the last chapter: **vulnerability**. One of the barriers that can come between children and parents is trust. I know it may seem counterintuitive to some, but it has been my experience that an essential part of the trust our family enjoys with one another is our willingness to be vulnerable with one another. And being the parents, it was up to me and Mary Jo to model that first for our kids. They need to know we aren't perfect either. Tell them about your struggles. Ask their forgiveness when you have hurt them or let them down. When you are frustrated or angry, explain what you want for them and how this issue is working against that. Your heart for them is good: even when—maybe especially when—you're angry. Let them see your heart. Tell them stories about when you were a kid and made a regrettable choice. When you have something you need to own, model what it looks like for a beloved son of God to own his guilt while being secure in his belovedness. If we try to present to our kids anything else, it won't be long and they will first be suspicious and then just plain dismissive. They know better. And if we want our kids to trust us, they have to know we are also growing and learning. And they need to know that the life of the beloved is a lifelong journey.

5) The fifth tool is **celebration**. Yes, we have a responsibility to confront and help our kids "tend the soil" to reshape their soft character. Our kids need parents who know how to lovingly,

wisely, and patiently discipline and teach. But our kids also need encouragement and affirmation for those moments that the fruit of firm character blossoms in their lives. When my daughter was a freshman in high school, she had a moment that her mother and I still treasure. While taking a test, she approached the teacher to ask a question. While there, another student turned in a test and, inadvertently, Ellie saw one of the answers given on the test. It was a question my daughter thought she would have been able to answer for herself, but having seen another student's response, she no longer felt confident that her work was her own. She finished the test and, as she turned it in, told the teacher what had happened and said she didn't think she should get credit for the answer she gave. She came home from school and shared that story with her mother and me while feeling a little bummed about what that would mean for her grade. Yes, it was a bummer that her grade would suffer, but come on! How incredible was that? It was an extremely difficult invitation for a 14-year-old girl to move toward. But she did! She recognized the invitation in the moment. She weighed and completely understood the cost of moving toward it. She chose it anyway. That was gardening the soil of her heart, and the "good soil" yielded the fruit of honesty and integrity, fruit that has only grown more through the years. Now on the verge of her own initiation, it is one aspect of God's firm character she beautifully reflects back to the world.

God is at work. He is growing Christlikeness in us, growing us up for the life he designed for us to live. It was a life Jesus modeled in his life on this earth. As sons and daughters fully adopted into his family, it is a life we inherited as well. He is growing us to live our lives guided by wisdom, uncompromising in loyalty, inspired by freedom, motivated by oneness, and firm in character. It all comes together in one more thing.

Love.

DRIVEN BY LOVE

"A new command I give you: Love one another. As I have loved you, so you must love one another. By this everyone will know that you are my disciples, if you love one another" (John 13:34, 35).

The culmination of the life God designed for us builds to love. God is love, and everything he does is driven by his pure, inexhaustible, unfathomable love. As image-bearers, the full scope of God's love is what we were designed to reflect—back to him and to each other. It is what a life guided by the elements laid out in this chapter collectively builds to. Love is the ultimate end of all God's work, the pinnacle characteristic of the life he designed for us.

The context for Jesus' words in John's gospel is sobering. He said many things to his disciples that night as they shared one last meal before his arrest. Though he'd told them what was coming, they still didn't quite seem to get it. He'd tried to prepare them but, around that table, they didn't fully understand the ordeal in front of them. John, though, would remember that night vividly. Years later he would capture the events in his gospel, the weight of Jesus' words now fully appreciated. On the eve of his crucifixion, Jesus was imparting the things he most desperately wanted his followers to take away from all they had experienced in their three years together. In that context he says: "Love one another." But that's not all. He adds, *"As I have loved you, so you must love one another."* Then, to really drive the point home, he declares love as the defining characteristic of all who follow him. Love—our capacity to reflect Jesus' love back to God and to each other—is to be our calling card. How did Jesus love?

*In your relationships with one another,
have the same mindset as Christ Jesus:*

Who, being in very nature God,

*did not consider equality with God something
to be used to his own advantage;*

*rather, he made himself nothing by taking
the very nature of a servant,*

being made in human likeness.

And being found in appearance as a man,

he humbled himself

by becoming obedient to death—

even death on a cross!

(Philippians 2:5-8)

I never get tired of reading those words from Paul. Every time I reflect on what Jesus did—setting aside the glory of his heavenly throne, immersing himself in the full human experience, including the bitterness of betrayal and rejection, and, finally, submitting to humiliating death at the hands of his own creation he came to rescue—I sit in humble awe. Jesus didn't just love. He was *driven* by it. His is an uncompromising, sacrificial, deeply passionate, fiercely intentional love. And, he says to you and me, this is how we are to love as well.

There is a reason this is the last work we look at. Everything we've looked at comes together in one thing—*the* thing! There is a beautiful progression and overlap that emerges with each facet. It all starts with living in ever more intimacy with our heavenly Father while

> His is an uncompromising, sacrificial, deeply passionate, fiercely intentional love. And, he says to you and me, this is how we are to love as well.

learning to recognize, hear, and heed his wise counsel. Maturity and resilience grow as we learn to walk intimately with him in authentic, uncompromising loyalty through the storms of life. Freedom is the result as we receive healing that breaks the grip of fear and shame. The life and love of the Father give birth to new hearts that cry "Abba" while mirroring his motivation for intimacy and oneness. Out of that oneness, our hearts become fertile ground for the fruit of firm character. The fruit of that firm character is then reflected back to him and the world around us. All the wisdom we are learning to live by, our uncompromising loyalty through difficult circumstances, the freedom we have and are learning to live in, all of our battles for oneness, the character that God is growing in us—it all builds and comes together in our ability and capacity to love. The more God frees us for what is most true, the more we are able to love the way Jesus does!

It is love that rescued me in the wreckage of my crash and burn. It is love that landed me in the wilderness. It is love that called out to me and compelled me to stay, and then venture deeper. It is love that kept me moving forward even when disoriented and disillusioned. It is love that gave and continues to give me the courage to face, and eventually overcome, my shame and fear. It is love that led me to understand a vision for my family, and it is love that has carried us each step of the way, a journey that's taken us well more than a decade. It is love that pulled Ben through the storm of his senior year. It is love that propels us through this final year of Ellie's initiation journey and the early years of Ian's journey.

It is love that compelled you to pick up this book, an act of a man with a good father's heart and profound love for his children. It is love that inspires you to drive a stake in the ground and turn against the current of generational momentum. It is love that has you ready to embark on your own initiation journey for your kids and family, a journey measured in years!

It is love that compels a father of grown children to courageously turn away from the tyranny of regret and shame and pursue reconciliation with his children. It is love that inspires us to bring our good father's heart to the world. It is love: passionate, roll-up-your-sleeves, never-give-up, fiercely intentional love. And it is glorious. This, beloved son, is the weight and strength of your life that you are beginning to understand. It is the weight and strength of your children's lives that you are training and preparing them for. We are image-bearers, and our heavenly Father is most definitely up to something. He is working, and all his work is growing us up for the life he designed us to live. In freeing us for what is most true, he is freeing us to reflect his love back to him and his creation. You, your wife, your children—all of you are destined to be a powerful force for good, a beacon of love that all the forces of evil cannot overcome. This is a reality that will make the enemy tremble. It is glorious love.

And as we'll discuss in the next and final chapter, it is our purpose.

Next: We have come a long way, beloved son. As he fathers you, so you are learning to father your children. Now everything comes together as we explore the purpose we share in living that life. You have an irreplaceable part to play in this very big story.

Chapter Ten

PURPOSE

"Teacher, which is the greatest commandment in the Law?" Jesus replied: "'Love the Lord your God with all your heart and with all your soul and with all your mind.' This is the first and greatest commandment. And the second is like it: 'Love your neighbor as yourself.' All the Law and the Prophets hang on these two commandments" (Matthew 22:36-40).

Start children off on the way they should go, and even when they are old they will not turn from it (Proverbs 22:6).

The whole week I felt like a kid at Christmas as we counted down the days to Ben's initiation ceremony. With each passing day it became more and more difficult to contain the emotion. It was a week of joyful reflection as I looked back on ten years of journeying with God into an adventure that grew out of failure, rejection, disillusion, and despair. I reflected on the unsettling and disorienting crash and burn that started it all. I remembered the painful and systematic undoing that, bit by bit, stripped me of everything I believed I needed to stand before God and man unashamed. I was overcome with humble gratitude as I relived the night my friend helped me see the obvious when he pointed me toward a full embracing of fatherhood.

I remembered how God fathered me in those early days—gently and, at times, comically, confronting me with a simple and incredibly uncomfortable question that forced me to say, over and over, that I was a full-time dad. It was a loving, tender, painful, and intensely personal healing from my wise and loving Father, a healing that opened the door for everything that followed for me and my family. I looked back with unspeakable pride and joy at the man my little boy had become. I drank in the memories of the day of his birth, the awe and joy we experienced with each milestone: smiling, crawling, walking, talking. I remembered his birthdays, teaching him to read, playing with him, watching him make friends, play sports, and learn to ride his bike. I thought about his growth from a baby to a toddler to a little boy. I remembered his preschool years that gave way to kindergarten. I marveled at just how fast the years went by; the grade school years were over way too soon. I remembered my son's baptism, a nine-year-old boy full of life and love who, in simple childlike trust, started a journey into the unknown with me. The teenage years were here and gone even faster. I remembered the joy of the ceremony that marked his transition into those years.

Each memory was a celebration shared with God. I relived key moments of growth and failure, triumph and confusion, clarity and uncertainty, confidence and doubt, a deeply personal and intimate journey shared by father and son, mother and son, father and mother. I especially felt the sacred weight of the final year we had shared together, a refining crucible for each of us in preparation for this long-awaited moment. Ten years had changed me as a man, husband, and father. Ten years had changed Mary Jo as a woman, wife, and mother. And ten years had changed my son into a man ready to stand on his own two feet as a beloved son of God. Yeah. It was an emotional week.

It all built to the climactic moment on the day of his initiation. After many days of reflection and emotional buildup, I was a bundle of nerves. Finally, the long anticipated moment came. I describe the ceremony itself and the entire knighthood model in Appendix A of this book, so I won't get into those details here. What I do want to share, as best I can, is the overwhelming power and joy of the moment. There we were experiencing this milestone, just as I had first imagined a decade earlier. I was overcome with emotion as I looked into the eyes of my son standing before me, his grandfather, and his uncles. I was unable to finish the blessing I had prepared to share with him and speak over him. I had to offer that to him later—but that didn't matter. I gathered myself enough to move on. I stood in awe as we reached the crowning moment we had come so far to share: my son kneeling before me as I knighted him and officially initiated him into manhood. I do not have the words to adequately describe just how powerful and utterly divine all of it was. We all know of the disappointing experience that comes with buildup, hype, and anticipation for something significant only to have the actual moment fall short of expectations. Well, this was not one of those times! Ten years of anticipation, buildup, and preparation weren't enough to prepare me for the actual experience. It was that powerful, and it is an experience I long for you and your family to know for yourselves.

And you can.

Believe me, I know how daunting it can be to stand at the beginning of a journey measured in years. It is a sobering experience to say the least. So let's pause a minute to come back to where we started. Way back in the first chapter, our journey began with the recognition of the secret burden men just like you have been living with. You picked up this book because, as a good man and a good father, you are very aware of your sacred role and the divine responsibility you have for your kids and family. You have done your best every day to offer your heart, love, encouragement, and presence. You have coached your kids' teams, helped them with homework, and done your part to provide for them. You have delighted over them and been perplexed by them. You have encouraged, disciplined, taught, listened, played, cried, laughed, and cheered. Still, in spite of all you offer every day, you have been haunted by the fear that it has not, and never will be, enough. Add to that a culture that offers little in the way of encouragement to men and fathers and the secret burden you've been living with becomes even heavier.

It is a burden I know all too well. It is what fueled my passionate plea to God all those years ago to understand his design for fatherhood, and it is why I've shared my story with you through this book. Yes, the invitation in front of you now is into an epic adventure with God—wherever you are in your fatherhood journey. What lies ahead is long and challenging and will require no small amount of perseverance and courage.

But it's important to say once more: *you can do this.*

Failure and regret are not inevitable. There is hope, there is a design for fatherhood, and, now, you have begun to learn it and understand it. You can flourish as a dad for your children and family. You can foster intimacy with your children, shepherd them through the ups and downs of life, bestow a deep sense of sacred identity, and initiate them into adulthood. Older men can step out into a journey of reconciliation as you offer your restored and healing father's heart to your older or grown children. You can offer your strength and encouragement as you drive a stake in the ground to turn against the current of generational momentum. Healing, wholeness, and redemption await as you courageously follow God's invitation.

As important as it is to be inspired by the promise of what lies ahead, I also want to offer encouragement by taking a moment to look back and reflect. A journey of a thousand miles starts with a single step. Let's not overlook the fact that you have already taken those crucial first steps! We do have a bit more ground to cover to see the completed picture of God's work in our lives. But it helps to pause a moment to reflect on what you have already done.

The journey you have been on began because of something that had been stirring and awakened in you long before you picked up any book. It was your good father's heart that has had you eager to understand more clearly your calling as a dad, to confront your secret burden of fear. The first thing to celebrate and be encouraged by is your good father's heart that moved toward that fear. Many run from it. Many numb it. Many ignore it and simply continue taking their best guess at fathering. Many of those men still offer wonderful things, but they also go through all their years of influence never really understanding their calling. You wanted more. So you responded with vulnerability and humility and began your search to more fully understand your responsibility. You picked up a book to see what another man's story might offer for that search. What you found were invitations. Some of those invitations were difficult—and surprising. Still, you continued moving toward them, even when you realized the invitations were not, at first, for your children at all. Instead you found an invitation for an initiation of your own! It was a step into something new, unique, and unknown. It may not have been what you expected, but you moved toward it anyway—again, compelled by your good father's heart.

More invitations awaited you, invitations to begin understanding your story. The way forward was through going back. You courageously began to acknowledge the impact of the past, wounds and messages, especially in defining moments with your own dad, that have had a profound impact on the man you are today. Within that was another difficult invitation to exercise vulnerability and allow yourself to grieve, maybe for the first time, as you started the healing process, a process that may be just beginning and is quite probably still unfolding. You also moved toward invitations to "know your enemy," learn his schemes, his target, and the agreements he is always angling for. Then you moved toward another invitation to resist, fight, and ultimately learn how to win—to stand your ground with courageous resolve as you have started breaking agreements reinforced by years of illusion. You have moved toward invitations to unlearn old assumptions to make room for new understanding, healing your perception of God and his true heart toward you. That has also opened doors of healing your perception of yourself.

And all of that before we even started talking about your children!

You kept going. You understood all that was about your children! You understood that you could not give what you, yourself, did not have. So you embraced a principle that will now shape every day of the journey ahead: as you are being fathered, so you will father your children. The life of intimate sonship that has now begun for you, then, is the strength and source of all you will turn and offer your family. You have begun to understand God's design for fatherhood: a calling to your divine responsibility to bestow sacred identity to your kids and family: that they are loved, they belong, and they have nothing to prove. It is the kind of love and delight every child is made to want and need from their father—and the truth is, we never grow out of it. The desire is divine. When they are young, your kids look to you and their mother to satisfy that desire. That is a good thing. It is the design. It is also the design that, on their journey to adulthood, you would teach them, prepare them, and train them to receive that sense of sacred identity from the primary source. This is the intentionality of initiation, and this is the divine responsibility God has invited you into as a father.

Your understanding of your responsibility then grew as you explored a vision for the work God is doing in each of us, growing us up for the life he designed for us. It is a life he very much intends for us to understand. It is the life he is fathering us into and, at the same time, invites us to partner with him in fathering our children into as well.

Whew!

That, beloved son, is not a journey for the faint of heart! But this is the thing I find most inspiring of all. All of that was just so you can start something, an initiation journey for you and your family that is measured in years! That is an incredibly courageous demonstration of love!

There's one more important group to discuss.

Not all who have come this far still have young children at home. Some of you are in a very different stage of your fatherhood journey. You too have ventured this far so you can now start something no less inspiring: a journey of intentional fatherhood with your grown kids and grandkids. That is an inspiring act of love from a man who simply refuses to let shame and regret have the final word for him and his children. Your fatherhood journey is nowhere close to being done. Yes, your years of influence when your children were young are behind you. It would be so easy to fade into the background and assume you have nothing left to offer. But not you. You have allowed your father's heart to dream and hope again as you have taken a stand of holy defiance and refused to accept the lie that it's too late to make a difference. You are determined to go forward from here as you offer your strength, wisdom, and growing understanding in sacrificial love and service to your family. For some of you that involves a difficult road of reconciliation—also a journey that may be measured in years! Whatever the nature of your relationship with your adult children, it is not too late, and your resolve to move forward with God is also an incredibly courageous demonstration of love that, rest assured, shakes the cosmos as all of Heaven roars (see Hebrews 12:1-3)!

Whatever your story, the fact that you are here is cause for celebration and encouragement. No, that's not quite right. It demands it! You have taken weeks or even months to invest deeply in your own heart and story. You have invested your heart, strength, courage, and goodness into the ongoing fight for your own healing, understanding, and freedom so you could then turn and engage in the fight for the hearts of your family. And you are doing it to give something precious and priceless to them, something you probably never had yourself. That is a man who knows how to love well, and a man who is already living out his purpose.

Everything we have discussed and explored points each man, woman, and child to their destiny. There is a strength and weight to each of our lives, something you are beginning to understand, a grasping that you will bestow to your children. So let's dig in one more time to complete the picture by understanding the purpose for the work God is doing in our lives.

PURPOSE

We, therefore, are Christ's <u>ambassadors</u>,
as though God were making his appeal through us
(2 Corinthians 5:20, emphasis mine).

Paul's letters to the Corinthians tell a story of a rather dysfunctional community. Through his two letters he addresses unsavory political power plays, sex scandals, tribalism, arrogance, pride, greed, and selfishness, among other things. In the midst of his truth-telling, he contrasts the rampant dysfunction with a hopeful and inspirational reminder of the purpose they have inherited as followers of Jesus. The small stories in which they are living become painfully apparent when he reminds them of the epic story and their place in it—to take their place with God on the front lines in the fight against the enemy by living as ambassadors to the world around them. It is a call back to the original design.

Then God said, "Let us make mankind in our image, in our
likeness, so that <u>they may rule</u> over the fish in the sea and the birds
in the sky, over the livestock and all the wild animals, and over all
the creatures that move along the ground"
(Genesis 1:26, emphasis mine).

The original design, your purpose and mine, is to *rule*! So it is the case for each of us that we are born with a kingdom of our own. We all have people, places, responsibilities, ideas, and desires that, together, make up our own kingdom over which to rule. We have authority and influence and, as the sixteenth-century philosopher and mathematician Blaise Pascal said, "the dignity of causality in our world." We navigate our days and exercise authority over our kingdoms, our choices big and small determining the trajectory of our days. Ruling, however, in and of itself, is not the entire scope of our purpose. Yes, ruling is something we all do. However, ruling according to the original design . . . well, that's something we are learning to do. The original design always has been for each of us to rule with God. This is our true purpose. So much of what we have explored together—the entire aim of initiation—is an invitation into intimate sonship with him. Everything else emanates from a restored and healing relationship with God. That is the context in which we were made to rule.

Sound familiar? As he fathers you, so you father your children.

That is the context, then, for Paul's words to the Corinthians as he reminds them of their—and our—purpose: to be Christ's ambassadors. An ambassador is one sent by an authority as his or her official representative, one who bears the authority of the one who sent them. God sends us in the authority of his name and kingdom to represent him and his goodness and faithfulness in *our* kingdom! Think about that for a minute! God has chosen to send you as his official representative! But who does he send us to?

Your good father's heart and the weight of your life, beloved son, is given to you by God, first and foremost, for your children and family. By no means, however, is it only for them. The world needs your father's heart. Your kids need it. Your wife needs it. Your neighbors, brothers, sisters, friends, coworkers, parents—your kingdom needs your good father's heart and it needs a man prepared to embrace and fulfill his purpose to this world around us. We are given authority as his ambassadors, entrusted and commissioned to bring the full authority of his kingdom over our kingdom and rule with him. The more you learn to live the life of the beloved, the more you carry the kingdom of God. In other words, where you go, God's kingdom goes.

We are ambassadors, and we were made to rule.

But still, what does that mean?

Jesus, when he was asked that question, brilliantly answered when confronted by a Pharisee who was another in a long line of many trying to embarrass and trap the Rabbi. Certain he had Jesus cornered, the religious leader asked:

> *"Teacher, which is the greatest commandment in the Law?" Jesus replied: "'Love the Lord your God with all your heart and with all your soul and with all your mind.' This is the first and greatest commandment. And the second is like it: 'Love your neighbor as yourself.' All the Law and the Prophets hang on these two commandments"* (Matthew 22:36-40).

Genius.

In a moment the Pharisee expected would embarrass Jesus, he took a seemingly impossible question and, to everyone's amazement, summarized the heart of the entire law and laid bare the original design—and with it provided a brilliantly clear understanding of the purpose we were made to live out.

Jesus said the first and most important law is to love the Lord your God with all your heart, soul, mind, and strength. The second is to love your neighbor as yourself. In the last chapter we looked at a vision for the work God is doing in each of us: growing us up for the life he designed each of us to live. We learned that love is the outcome of all of God's work. It's what everything builds to, and it is our purpose.

Let's tie all this together. You, beloved son, were made to be a powerful force for good. You, your children, your wife—each man, woman, and child, each of us, are made to be a powerful force for good by being an ambassador, a kingdom bearer, one bringing the full authority of his kingdom over ours as we rule with him by:

1) **Knowing God as he wants to be known.** A heavenly Father whose heart toward us is so very good and who passionately pursues deep intimacy, oneness, with his sons and daughters.

2) **Knowing myself as he wants me to be known.** Notice that the commandment reads: "Love your neighbor as yourself." In my experience, that link is, at best, overlooked. Worse is how that link is often misunderstood. Worse still is the far too common tendency to dismiss it all together. So I invite you to look at it and sit with it once again. "Love your neighbor as *yourself*." The implication cannot be dismissed. The love I have and offer for others is a direct outpouring of the love I have for myself. We find ourselves face to face with a fundamental truth we have addressed many times in this book: You cannot give what you don't have. As a father, then, the love you offer your family will flow out of the love you have for yourself. This is why we spent so much time on your initiation into intimate sonship. You, beloved son, are learning to be a fathered son. And as we have said, as you are being fathered, so you will father your children. If you are going to embrace and fulfill the promise of fatherhood to bestow a deeply rooted sense of identity to your children as beloved sons and daughters, you must first be rooted in your own belovedness. This means living deeply and growing ever deeper roots in the ultimate reality that you are deeply, completely, and unconditionally loved, that you belong, and that you have nothing to prove. As you are fathered into that truth, so you will father your children and live out your purpose as a kingdom bearer in every sphere of your life.

3) **Loving those around me as he wants me to love them.** Finally, we come to the fullness of our purpose: "Love your neighbor." To be a powerful force for good as I carry the kingdom wherev-

er I go with fiercely intentional, unwavering, sacrificial, radical, generous love. The same way I am loved, the same way I have found belonging, and the same way I am learning that I have nothing to prove.

This is the purpose that Jesus lived, and it is the same purpose we were made to fulfill. The enemy trembles in the face of a fully initiated man or woman of God. He simply cannot withstand the weight and strength of a man or woman living deeply from their sacred identity, intimately fathered and grown up for the life the Father designed for each of us to live, and living out the purpose we were made to fulfill.

This is what it looks like to love well. Exactly what you have been doing one invitation at a time through each chapter of this book.

It is the heart of a man embracing his calling of fatherhood.

And it is a sight to behold.

FINAL BLESSING

The picture is now complete. From the heart of one father to another, I eagerly look forward to what lies ahead for you and your family. There is so much in front of you now. Many of you will begin looking ahead to a journey of initiation that will take years to realize. Between now and that very special day, you and your family have so much to experience and learn, to laugh about and cry about, to be joyful about and sad about. You will be confused at times, and you will see things very clearly at times. There are times the road will seem easy, and there will be times the journey will seem very hard. Through it all, God will be working in you, your wife, and your children. There will be times you will hurt one another and have to forgive one another. But you'll forgive, learn, pick each other up, and keep going—and it will all be worth it.

Others of you, older men whose years of influence have passed, now look forward to a different journey of service and sacrificial love to your adult children and grandchildren. Your fatherhood journey is far from over! Your father's heart has been awakened, and you have courageously broken your agreement with the lie that it is too late for you. You too have driven a stake in the ground and taken a stand against the current of generational momentum. It is an act of profound love on behalf of your grown children. There is, of course, no guarantee that your kids will readily receive what you offer, but you're offering your heart and strength anyway. It is truly inspiring. No, you cannot recover your years of influence and recapture what you missed. You can, however, offer your strength, wisdom, and encouragement to invite your grown children into their own initiation with God and launch their own initiation journey with their kids. It all stems from your good father's heart, the heart of a man who knows how to love. It is a heart, whether they respond to it or not, that your children still very much want and need.

Whatever your path, it is a journey of a thousand miles. The hope for what lies ahead will be a beacon pulling you forward. But it is also important to remember how you will get there: a fiercely intentional, daily faithfulness to take that next step with God as he fathers you and, in so doing, gives you everything you need to father your children. Together, you will move through the ordinary day-to-day, moment-by-moment experiences of life, walking intimately with God and each other. Bit by bit, it will all add up to something indescribably extraordinary.

Your divine responsibility is to bestow sacred identity. With that point clear, men, we start with the end in mind. God is growing you to take hold of the full weight of who you are: beloved son and kingdom bearer. You are a powerful force for good. As you learn to embrace the full weight of your life, you now bring your heart, alive and free, to your most sacred role: fatherhood. The enemy trembles in the wake of all who find their way to living in the ultimate reality of their sacred identity. You are finding your place in the great story and, now, also beginning to understand what it looks like to usher your children to their place in that story. You are raising beloved sons and cherished daughters. You are raising kingdom bearers. You are done playing it small. It is a new day for you and your family, the destiny of a thousand generations forever changed.

We have come a long way together. From one father to another, I am honored that you would allow me to share my story with you. And I'm honored to share in this extraordinary calling of fatherhood with you. As we come to the end of this particular road, I leave you with a last thought, one inspired, once again, by *The Lord of the Rings: Two Towers*.

We drew inspiration from the movie before as we looked at the people of Rohan, having fled to the fortress of Helm's Deep, finding themselves face to face with an enemy they'd hoped would never come. But the enemy did come, and with the sole purpose of murder and total destruction. So the people of Rohan mustered all the courage they could and stood valiantly in defiance of the intimidating evil before them. It all builds to an eerie silence, a tenuous calm as the imminent battle is about to begin.

It was a desperate moment that stemmed from the fateful decision of King Theoden for Rohan to retreat to Helm's Deep in the first place. Once the decision was made, however, events began to unfold that would inevitably lead to the deadly confrontation with the enemy. In the hurried mayhem after King Theoden's order, the king's niece, Eowyn, begins preparing for the march to Helm's Deep as she pulls her sword out of storage. It becomes quite clear that she is no mere novice as she draws the blade from the scabbard and begins to expertly wield her weapon. It is clear that she is prepared for the difficult road ahead. The Ranger, Aragorn, having noticed, approaches unseen and surprises her as she spins and swings downward, striking his outstretched blade.

"You have some skill with a blade!" he tells her.

As Eowyn frees her blade from Aragorn's, she displays some defiance.

"Women of this country learned long ago that those without swords may still die upon them," she says. "I fear neither death nor pain."

Honoring her courage, Aragorn respectfully asks: "What do you fear, my lady?"

She answers, with profound clarity: "A cage. To stay behind bars until use and old age accept them and all chance of valor has gone beyond recall or desire."

Aragorn is moved by her honor. "You are a daughter of kings," he says. "A shieldmaiden of Rohan. I do not think that will be your fate."[1]

Beloved son, I know what you fear. A fate of regret and failure: your years of influence spent carrying the weight of a divine responsibility with only your best guess as to how to embrace and fulfill it. To come to the end of the road, utterly spent, never having truly understood your sacred role and calling to your children, the promise of fatherhood unfulfilled.

To that I say this.

You are a beloved son of the King. A skilled swordsman and kingdom bearer. A powerful force for good with the heart and skills to embrace and fulfill the promise of fatherhood.

I do not think that will be your fate.

You . . . are an intentional dad.

NEXT STEPS

Okay, now what? That is an excellent question, and I'm glad you asked! I do have a few suggestions.

At the top of the list: sit back, reflect, and take a moment to celebrate what you've begun. As you sit with Jesus, it is very possible that he will begin to reveal what's next for you.

Here I offer a few thoughts of my own.

- Share this book with your wife. Yes, the book is written from one father to another. However, initiation is best done—actually, designed to be done—in full partnership with your wife. I am aware that writing to you as my primary audience could be a barrier for some women, leading some to believe that this isn't relevant for them. This could not be further from the truth and, if your wife does have that impression, rest assured this is not my intention. Parenting is a holy task for both husband and wife. To that end, I point you back to the prologue at the beginning of the book. This would be a good time to share the "Invitation to Moms." It was written to help you invite your wife into the journey, communicate my heart for her in writing this book, the relevance of these ideas for her and her sacred role of motherhood, and the journey of initiation that you are made to share together.

- Share the book with another man. Even young men who don't yet have children secretly live with the burden of knowing their responsibility but struggle to understand how to embrace and fulfill it. Who are some other men in your life longing to understand the divine responsibility of fatherhood?

- Share the book with your dad or other older men, or with your grown children. An untold story that has happened behind the scenes through the writing of this book is what has unfolded for me and my dad. As I began to write, I invited him to share in the process. I didn't know what to expect when I first extended that invitation. What God had in store was breathtaking as we've shared our lives and found understanding, healing, and reconciliation—something we have both waited decades to realize. This could very well be something God has in store for you as well.

- Go to theintentionaldad.org or scan the QR code at this end of this short section to subscribe to The Intentional Dad newsletter.

- Consider becoming a member of The Intentional Dad community. The Intentional Dad is an online community of fiercely intentional men and their families on a journey to embrace and fulfill the promise of fatherhood. Go to theintentionaldad.org or scan the QR code to find out how to subscribe and join. Here we will offer additional resources to help you in your journey.

- Begin the initiation journey with your kids. Start by looking at the knighthood model we have used for our family (Appendix A). Perhaps it is a model you want to use. Or maybe it will inspire you to imagine a different initiation model for your family.

- Still not sure what's next? Interested in starting the initiation journey but need more help understanding what that might look like for you and your family? Or maybe you are needing help understanding your own story? More individualized opportunities and resources can be found through The Intentional Dad community.

These are just a few suggestions you might consider for your next steps. The journey of a thousand miles happens one step at a time. I am truly excited for all that you and your family will share together on the road ahead, and I join all of Heaven in cheering you on each step of the way.

Onward!

Scan to go to theintentionaldad.org

Appendix A

KNIGHTHOOD MODEL FOR INITIATION

If you're at all like me, now that you have started walking the road of your own initiation, a new desire has already started growing alongside it. By now you have come to understand the pattern of fatherhood. You have clarity for the work he is doing in you and, therefore, you also have clarity for your sacred role and divine responsibility to your children: to partner with God in ushering your kids to adulthood as men and women who know who they are, to whom they belong, and who have been "trained to overcome all things" as adults fully equipped and prepared for a life of intimacy as apprentices of Jesus. Initiation is the fiercely intentional process by which that happens. As we discussed in chapter 3, the concept of initiation is hardly new. To those of us raised in modern Western culture, however, it is extremely new—perhaps even odd. But you are here now with the same question that started to arise in me all those years ago: *What does initiation look like for my family today?*

Like you, what I really was eager to discover was a vision for something I could lead my family into. There are many traditions for initiation through human history. You may even be awakening to a tradition you know has been part of your own lineage and cultural history.

Some Native American cultures, for example, have a long and rich tradition called a Vision Quest. The Jewish culture has the rich tradition of Bar and Bat Mitzvah. Those are just two examples. Regardless of the practice, all initiation traditions have some extremely important elements in common. All require the intentional preparation of the child leading to affirmation from the adult community in a sacred ceremony to seal a key stage of development. Initiation traditions also leverage the power of symbolism to capture the significance of the moment shared by the child and the community, symbolism that visually captures the core values that give definition to the transcendent life that binds them. These were all ideas that started to capture my imagination and, I hope and pray, are now beginning to capture yours as well. But, again, this is all totally new for most Westerners. Like you, I needed some inspiration to help me see and understand a model that could carry the vision for me and my family—something I knew that I, my wife, and my kids could see and understand.

As my desire for a clear vision for an initiation model started to grow, I came across a book titled *Raising a Modern-Day Knight* by Robert Lewis. It is Lewis's story, alongside two other men, as they set out on a journey to initiate their sons using the framework of knighthood. Lewis described what he and his friends learned about the medieval path to knighthood.

> Just as [a knight's] chivalry embodied a well-defined set of ideals, his life also outlined a well-defined process. The boy who pursued knighthood followed a clearly marked path.
>
> At age seven or eight, he became a page. He was removed from his mother's care and went to live in a castle, usually with an overlord or relative. Here, the page learned about armor and weapons and falconry, the rudiments of knighthood. He also performed household tasks for the "queen of the castle."
>
> At the age of 14, the page became a squire. He attached himself to a knight and traveled everywhere in his company, serving him in the most menial of tasks: he carried the knight's lance,

woke him in the morning, and even helped him dress. The squire also competed in tournaments and perfected the skills he had learned as a page. Such rigorous discipline prepared him for the final stage of his journey.

When he turned 21, he was eligible for knighthood. An elaborate initiation, which included a night-long vigil, a ceremonial bath, and a dubbing marked the completion of the process. He was now . . . *a knight!* He took his place in the order of knighthood and pledged himself to uphold the code of honor.

From page to squire to knight—a young man could envision the process, count the cost, and pursue his dream.[1]

This "well-defined process" is exactly what I had been searching for. The three stages of pagehood, squirehood, and knighthood captured my imagination in the intentionality of the process, the ideals of knighthood and, very importantly, a framework I could reimagine for me and my family in the twenty-first century.

So I did begin reimagining. God had been fathering me and teaching me. He had given me the clarity I had longed for in understanding his work in growing Christlikeness in me and, with it, clarity for my sacred role and divine responsibility to partner with him in the work of training, preparing, equipping, shepherding, and, ultimately, releasing my kids into adulthood. With the knighthood model, I had come across a well-defined process to instill and reinforce the foundational lessons of their sacred identities as God's beloved, a vision for understanding the work God is doing in fathering them, and understanding and living out their purpose as his beloved son/daughter. We began referring to this life of apprenticeship as the life of a warrior knight/warrior heroine. (That alone was extremely helpful in rooting our family in the reality of living in a universe at war.)

The framework of pagehood, squirehood, and knighthood is the framework I reimagined as a ten-year journey for each of my kids. Each stage is marked by a theme that defines the primary developmental focus of that period, a sacred ceremony for which they must prepare and in which the community of adults offers affirmation and celebration of the child and the milestone. It also provides rich tradition-worthy symbolism infused with deep meaning that captures the significance of the moment and the essence of the transcendent life as followers of Jesus that binds us. This, then, is what that has looked like for our family.

PRE-PAGEHOOD

The initiation journey actually begins before pagehood. Your children were all born with a divine desire to know that they are loved, they belong, and they have nothing to prove to earn that love. It is the kind of love and delight every child is made to want and need from you and their mother, and they never grow out of it. That is a good thing. It is the design. It is also the design that you would teach them, prepare them, and train them to receive and live from that sense of sacred identity directly from the primary source. That process begins, then, from conception as you and your wife together do your best to offer love, encouragement, belonging, direction, discipline, guidance, and security. You also begin the process of teaching them about God and his true heart for them. Gradually, these pre-pagehood years build a readiness for the official launch of the initiation journey.

For us, that transition began when our kids were 8 years old. That was the age they could begin to understand the journey to knighthood/heroinehood that I wanted to invite them to share with me. We began discussing the vision for a ten-year process of learning life as a follower of Jesus arm in arm with me. I began explaining the three stages of that journey and, especially, the stage of pagehood that would mark the official beginning of that journey. We started discussing identity, vision, and purpose to begin building familiarity with the language and an understanding of what it looks like to follow Jesus.

We began explaining life as an apprentice and the life of a warrior knight/heroine that God designed for them to live. Very importantly, this pre-pagehood stage was a time for them to understand that the initiation journey started with their own desire to live their lives as followers of Jesus.

With that desire awakened, I invited them to think about baptism. I explained the significance of baptism as something Jesus modeled and taught us to do, and that it was a moment to celebrate the start of their lives as his apprentice in an extremely special ceremony shared with family and friends. I was intentional from the beginning to help them understand that the invitation was into a significantly long journey of initiation with me and, more importantly, into a lifetime journey with God. It was an invitation that, of course, my wife and I really wanted them to accept. But it was also very important that they, as much as possible for an 8- or 9-year-old, understand what they would be saying yes to. Again, there are limitations of understanding at this age, but they are more than capable of knowing Jesus, his heart toward them, their need for him, and his invitation to live their lives intimately with him.

As Ben and Ellie have looked back, both have said that their understanding as pages was just a fraction of what they both know and understand now—which, of course, is the design. But they will also tell you that they understood they were saying yes to a lifetime journey with Jesus, that they had a basic understanding of what that looked like, and that they were saying yes to a God who loved them. Upon saying yes to Jesus—and yes to my invitation as well—we then began officially preparing for their baptism, the start of their lives of apprenticeship with Jesus, and, specifically, the start of their initiation journey as pages.

PAGEHOOD

THEME

In medieval times, a boy's path to knighthood would begin as a page. As a page, the boy started learning "about armor and weapons and falconry, the rudiments of knighthood." The theme that defines this developmental stage, then, is learning. In these years kids learn the concepts of identity, vision, and purpose, and not just in an intellectual sense (although that is certainly part of it). The learning that is most significant is in understanding the relevance of those ideas to their daily lives. As our children experienced life I would help them discern heart issues, revisit those, and remind them, in word and deed, of their sacred identities (often as in the "rolling eyes" thing!). I would help them understand how they were being fathered and "grown up" into Christlikeness and what it looks like to live out their purpose as kingdom bearers.

These opportunities would regularly present themselves in their relationships with their friends and siblings, in their successes and failures in school, sports, and activities, and in their interactions with me and their mom. It is one thing for you to begin teaching them about the beautiful reality of their sacred identities as God's beloved. It is quite another for them to learn that through all the realities, confusion, wonder, triumph, and disappointment that they experience every day. These are the years that they learn the actual experience of belovedness from you every time they fall into the safety of your loving arms. You build trust as you first offer them a safe place to grieve, wonder, ask questions, and reflect. They begin learning the work of guarding their hearts with wise, shame-free truth-telling, an acknowledgment of wounds, identification of messages, understanding just how real those messages feel, breaking of agreements the enemy was working to obtain, and, finally, with compassion, gentleness, and your strong assurance to remind them of the truth that will never be taken from them: they are loved, they belong, and they have nothing to prove. The pagehood years are when they learn these "rudiments of knighthood" as reality through your intentional fathering.

PREPARATION

The preparation for the pagehood ceremony was a time of study and discussion with me as I led them through an exploration of Scripture. It was a process that took ten to twelve weeks as we explored Scripture together (again, Scripture references available for your own exploration in Appendix C). We studied and discussed the foundational truth of identity. We explored the vision for the life of a warrior knight/heroine as we studied the life Jesus lived—the same life we were designed to live. We finished our preparation by studying and understanding our purpose as kingdom bearers. Our attention then turned to the ceremony itself. We discussed the significance of baptism, the start of their initiation journey, and what it meant to be a page.

CEREMONY

The pagehood ceremony is built around baptism; each of my kids was 9 at the time. Just as Jesus modeled, I baptized them in the same manner in which he was baptized, a dunk in the water as I described the symbolism of the baptism tradition exactly as Paul described it in Romans:

All of us who were baptized into Christ Jesus were baptized into his death. We were therefore buried with him through baptism into death in order that, just as Christ was raised from the dead through the glory of the Father, we too may live a new life
(Romans 6:3, 4; verse 3 is author's paraphrase)

That portion of the ceremony was very much like other baptism ceremonies. There were two aspects, however, that we incorporated that made it distinct. First, one thing that may be very different from many baptism ceremonies is the fact that I led the baptism. No, that wasn't just because I had been in ministry before and had been to seminary. It was essential as a recognition of my sacred role and divine responsibility I carry for my children as their father. I was taking up my calling by taking responsibility for all aspects of their initiation, something extremely important for me to demonstrate in my role in preparing my kids and then leading them through the actual ceremony.

The initiation journey is both an invitation from me to my kids and a promise from me to train them and be with them each step of the way. The ceremonies are extremely important moments that mark key milestones, something very much meant to be shared between father and child as he bestows sacred identity by leading and sharing the milestone with them. So, yes, I baptized my kids and, as I have had the privilege of coaching other men through preparing their own families for initiation, those men also led the baptism ceremony for their own kids. (I would also add that this, of course, is something that would be very appropriate for fathers and mothers to share in. At the time we did these ceremonies for our kids, baptism was not something Mary Jo felt comfortable doing, so she offered her support and encouragement as a proud mother observing and celebrating the moment. Other families, however, may want a ceremony in which the husband and wife baptize their child together.)

Secondly, before the actual baptism, I prepared my kids for a series of questions designed to help them express their understanding of the life of a warrior knight/heroine and life as an apprentice of Jesus. There were questions about the three foundational ideas we studied together for those ten to twelve weeks: Identity, Vision, and Purpose. They knew going into the ceremony what the questions were, and part of our preparation included practicing how they would answer. More important than simply giving a "right answer," though, was the work we did in developing their understanding behind their answers. So the ceremony began with me affirming, praising, and celebrating my son/daughter and the journey we had already shared to get ready for the moment. That led to the next phase of the ceremony, one in which I would ask them the questions that gave them the opportunity to express their understanding of the life to which they were saying yes. Next was the baptism itself, after which I also sealed the significance of the moment by declaring that their initiation journey had now begun—they had just entered life as a page.

SYMBOLISM

The ceremonies of initiation are essential in sealing key milestone moments of the journey. Just as important, though, is the rich tradition-worthy symbolism that accompanies the ceremony. The medieval tradition of the family crest provided an excellent opportunity to reimagine a new tradition for our family. I could have gone in search of old archives and possibly found an old "Manly" family crest. I may have discovered something really cool in my heritage had I done that, and some of you may choose to do that for yourselves. However, I saw an even greater opportunity: to have a new crest designed, one with symbolism that aligned with the training I led my kids through, symbolism that captured the essence of life as followers of Jesus that binds us. So I found someone to design a totally new "Manly family crest" in which every element symbolically captured our lives of apprenticeship with Jesus. This and each of the other symbols from the other ceremonies are pictured and further explained in Appendix B. For their baptism/pagehood ceremony, then, each of my children was given the gift of an elegantly framed copy of our family crest. Each of them now has this crest hanging prominently in their room. It is a daily reminder of who they are, to whom they belong, the work God is doing in fathering them, and the purpose we share as kingdom bearers.

SQUIREHOOD

THEME

The next phase on the path to knighthood is squirehood. As a squire, a boy would begin traveling with and serving his master. As a page, he was occupied with learning the "rudiments of knighthood." As a squire, he now began taking responsibility for the development of his skills as well as responsibility for life with his master. The theme of this stage, then, is responsibility. As a page, my children learned the foundational truths of identity, vision, and purpose both in study and, far more importantly, in the relevance of those truths to their everyday life. They also started learning basic spiritual disciplines like Bible reading, journaling, prayer, solitude, and service. The pagehood years are about exposure to "the rudiments of knighthood" for the purpose of learning. Squirehood marks a transition in which they begin learning to take responsibility for their lives with Jesus.

PREPARATION

Preparation for squirehood actually begins as a subtle transition during the pagehood years. As my children approached what I call the "age of responsibility" (around age 10), I began to explain to them the season of life they were entering, an age lovingly referred to as the "tween" years. It is a season of major transition as kids straddle that awkward in-between of a childhood they are beginning to leave behind and the responsibilities of the teen years that are just ahead. The intentionality of this transition was not only in their spiritual lives. The transition into the "years of responsibility" included preparation for and gradually increasing ownership of things like earning and spending money, homework, cleanliness and hygiene, conflict resolution, diet, and, yes, beginning to learn to take responsibility for their spiritual well-being. The squirehood years are marked by a continual growth in their capacity for responsibility. But it is not intended to be a hard and rapid transition. It is a gradual, age-appropriate transition that starts with helping the son/daughter become aware of the often confusing challenges of the tween years.

Starting at about age 10, they begin to experience a tug-of-war between the simple dependence and innocence of childhood and their growing desire for independence and autonomy. An essential part of the preparation for squirehood is helping to bring clarity to this confusing time and gradually offering them more and more experiences with being responsible. Sometimes my children would handle that responsibility well. Other times . . . well, not so much. But by starting that transition in the pagehood years, you are helping them make those mistakes in an environment in which consequences are minimized. They are still pages, which means they are learning. In this case, it is learning responsibility, and it is in preparation for the official transition to squirehood at the age of thirteen.

In preparation for the squirehood ceremony, my children each went through the same study and preparation we had done for their pagehood ceremony preparation. This time, though, they practiced responsibility by first taking time to study on their own. Afterward, we would we sit down together to discuss what God was teaching them, revisit ways they had experienced those things in their pagehood years, and talk about the ceremony and the significance of squirehood that would eventually lead to the final stage of knighthood/heroinehood. This would take, again, about ten to twelve weeks for us to work through. As a final step of preparation, I helped them get ready for a portion of the ceremony in which they would share what they learned as a page and how God had prepared them for squirehood.

CEREMONY

The responsibility of squirehood is about nurturing an increasing capacity to discern God's fathering in their lives. They learn more and more to discern God's voice and his invitations and, at the same time, to develop their capacity to guard their hearts against the schemes of the enemy. Again, this is not meant to be a harsh transition from the theme of learning in their pagehood years. It is an age-appropriate steady transition. That transition starts, however, with helping them understand that, as a squire, the time has come for them to learn how to seek out and recognize God's leading for themselves. It is an important change in mindset for the child, a change I wanted them to experience in the squirehood ceremony.

This ceremony, then, was intentionally done in "the wilderness." I looked for and found a forested area with some hiking trails. The location of the actual ceremony was not revealed to my kids. Instead, I had prepared six laminated cards (one for each of wisdom, loyalty, freedom, oneness, character, and love) and placed them along the trail that would lead them to the location where the ceremony would take place. For Ben, the ceremony started with him at the beginning of the trail with men praying over him. After the prayer, we gave his instructions and, after giving the men some time to go ahead to the final destination, he began walking the trail looking for the next laminated card.

On each of those cards I had taken time to write important words of affirmation and celebration for how I had seen God father him and how I had seen him grow in that area. Upon finding each card he read what I had written and then took some time for his own reflection with God. Then he would move on in search of the next card. The walk, then, became both an affirmation of his readiness of squirehood and a metaphor for squirehood in which he would now begin learning to look for and follow God's leading for himself along the "narrow road" of his life. After the sixth and final card he would venture a bit further until he arrived at the destination for the actual ceremony, where all of the men were waiting.

The ceremony began with each man lighting a candle and giving an unlit candle to my son. My son was given the opportunity to share with the men about the experience of walking the trail, anything he may have heard from God in that time, what he learned in his preparation for the ceremony, and his readiness for the next phase of initiation. Each man was given an opportunity to offer words of affirmation and blessing and, after we were finished, we brought our candle flames together to light Ben's candle, a symbolic community affirmation of his masculinity and readiness for squirehood. I then had him kneel as I offered words of celebration and affirmation, prayed over him, and finished with the declaration: "You knelt a page, now rise a squire." I presented him with his gift to mark the milestone.

The ceremony was the same for Ellie with one exception. As we continued living out this vision, our understanding and comfort with the ceremonies grew for me and my wife. As the years went on, my vision for how Mary Jo might be involved grew. So with the experience and learning from my son's ceremony, we now began the process of discerning how she could be involved in a way that she felt comfortable. For my daughter, the women, along with my wife, gathered at the final destination while the men gathered around Ellie at the start of the trail. After praying over her, we gave her instructions and asked her to wait while the men walked ahead to join the women at the final destination. For Ellie, we wanted the women to have the same opportunity to celebrate and affirm her femininity in the same way the men had affirmed and celebrated Ben's masculinity during his ceremony.

SYMBOLISM

During the ceremony the gift was kept out of sight, with my dad, until its conclusion. At that moment, he unveiled a shield hand-painted with the family crest (Appendix B) that he then handed to me, a generational bestowing of affirmation from grandfather to father, father to child. I presented it to my son/daughter and invited them to take hold as I explained the significance of the gift: a symbol for their lives as squires in which they would now learn to take responsibility for guarding their hearts as apprentices of Jesus.

KNIGHTHOOD/HEROINEHOOD

THEME

This is the crowning moment of a ten-year journey. To say it is a celebration is putting it mildly. What began at the age of 8 has steadily and intentionally prepared your child for this moment to affirm and celebrate their official initiation into adulthood.

With my children, through years of intentionality with their mother and me teaching, nurturing, guiding, correcting, urging, listening, praying, and discerning, they have been steadily ushered into the arms of their heavenly Father. The handoff complete, the moment has finally arrived to celebrate their standing before God as an adult fully prepared and trained to take full responsibility for their life of apprenticeship as a warrior knight/warrior heroine. For Ben, the affirmation the men offered him was a resounding answer to his most pressing question as a young man: "You have what it takes." Ellie will also have a theme for the affirmation we offer her. Her most pressing core question is subtly different, though: "You are enough, you are valued, and you are ready."

PREPARATION

Preparation for this ceremony is actually something that will be unique for each child. Through the years of squirehood, they have been steadily learning to take more and more responsibility for guarding their hearts, discerning God's voice and his invitations, resisting and overcoming the enemy, living ever more deeply from their sacred identities, and living out their purpose as kingdom bearers. That all builds to an extremely important final year in which Jesus finishes the work of initiation. As I described in chapter 9, the final work of initiation is something Mary Jo and I were never going to be able to complete. Everything we have invested in Ben and Ellie, and now Ian, was always leading to a hand-off. From the start, the goal of initiation was to prepare them to stand on their own before God as a fully capable and fully responsible adult. Their validation as an adult, then, always had to be something they experienced with and from God for themselves. There is no formula for this. My son was fathered through an intense season of suffering and warfare that stretched him to his limits. My daughter's experience has looked very different but is no less significant as God fathers her through her own fears and doubts—through the steady hand of her heavenly Father as she is being shaped into a resilient and confident woman.

As for my part, I also make a transition in this final year of preparation. This time, it is my job to come alongside them as a partner. We have regular check-ins that start with that all-important question: "How's your heart?" Together, we discover how God is fathering them, where he is working, where he is inviting them, and how the enemy is opposing them. I offer encouragement, discernment, prayer, understanding, shepherding, and coaching. In addition to all that, I also offer a reminder of where it is all headed, the triumphant moment of initiation, and the celebration ten years in the making. But the final leg of initiation is one they have to take for themselves. It is an incredibly important final year and, not surprisingly, it is opposed. There will be ups and downs, triumphs and discouragement. It is a challenging time for them, and it should be. It is a challenging time for me and their mother also, as we know we have to let go and trust. The preparation, then, is for each of us. It is challenging and yet it is worth it. Through it all they have a story of learning to take their first steps with God as an adult. It is a story they share and we celebrate during their ceremony.

As a final piece of preparation, I invite them to share, once again, in the same study preparation we did for pagehood and squirehood. It is good to come back to the foundational ideas but, more to the point, it actually leads to some reminiscing as we look back on the journey we've shared.

CEREMONY

Finally, the crowning moment comes. The ceremony for my son was a knighthood ceremony. I'll describe that one first.

KNIGHTHOOD

The ceremony took place in a private room we had prepared ahead of time. As we began, we consecrated (set apart as sacred) the moment. Afterward, the men went into the room without Ben, where we again prayed to consecrate this sacred portion of the ceremony in which the men had come together to affirm and bestow manhood to my son. After waiting a few moments to allow time for the prayer, my wife, who was waiting with my son outside, then released him into the room—the last time she would embrace him as a boy. He entered the room and stood before the men who had gathered to initiate him. We paused to be present to the sacred moment, and then I asked him to simply share his story, how God had fathered him, the significance of his final year, and the validation of his manhood he had received from God. Then his uncles, his grandpa, and I offered him blessing and affirmed his manhood while reinforcing the critical message: "You have what it takes." With the blessings offered, the men lit candles, and then all of us together lit Ben's candle, a symbolic bestowing of masculinity and manhood from us to him.

Then came the second portion of the ceremony: the knighting. The women joined us and, once there, we shared communion together. Then I asked Ben to kneel. My dad pulled out the custom-made sword he had been keeping out of sight and handed it to me. I turned and knighted my son, touching his right shoulder, head, and left shoulder as I charged him with living out his life as an apprentice of Jesus, as a warrior knight, and his purpose as a kingdom bearer. I finished the knighting by saying: "You knelt a squire, now rise a man, a beloved son of God, and a warrior knight." He stood, I handed him the sword, and I said, "Welcome to the ranks of warrior knights." I did not yet embrace him, however. We saved the first embrace for his mother; she was the first to embrace him on the day of his birth, now she would be the first to embrace him as a man.

HEROINEHOOD

At the time of the writing of this book, Ellie's initiation ceremony has not yet happened, but we are planning for it. Her ceremony will have many similarities to the knighthood ceremony, but there will be some differences to honor her femininity, her unique story and personality, and to honor some of her unique preferences. As we did with my son, we will start with prayer to consecrate the moment and, this time, we will also share communion together. Afterward, in a separate room just for the women, led by Mary Jo, they will take some time to bestow the blessing of affirmation of Ellie's womanhood. She will be invited to share her story, how God has fathered her through her journey, the significance of her final year, and the validation of the womanhood she has received from God. Then the women will have the opportunity to speak to Ellie and each offer their blessing, finishing with her mother's blessing. Then the women will light candles and, together, light Ellie's candle, a symbolic bestowing of femininity and and affirmation of womanhood from the women to her.

Then comes the moment of initiation. One of the distinctions for my daughter is the symbolism. More on that in a moment but, instead of a sword, she will be presented with a bow and arrows. So the initiation will begin with her little brother, Ian, presenting her with a quiver to hold the arrows. Then, Ben, her aunts and uncles, her grandparents, and then her mother and I will present her with the arrows. Affirmation and celebration of her readiness for womanhood will be offered in six blessings . . . a woman living the life of a warrior heroine marked by wisdom, loyalty, freedom, oneness, character, and love. After that I will share my blessing. I will then ask her to kneel. My dad will hand me her custom-made bow that he had been keeping out of sight. I will turn and touch her right shoulder, head, and left shoulder as I charge her with living out her life of apprenticeship as a warrior heroine and her purpose as a kingdom bearer. I will finish by saying: "You knelt a squire, now rise a woman, beloved daughter of God, and a warrior heroine." She will stand and I will hand her the bow as her mother welcomes her to adulthood with the words, "Welcome to the ranks of warrior heroines." Again, the first embrace will be with her mother, the first to embrace her on the day she was born, and now the first to embrace her as a woman. Then I will embrace her, the first man to embrace her as a woman.

SYMBOLISM

KNIGHTHOOD

The symbol for knighthood is, of course, a sword. I had one custom-made and etched with the defining characteristics of knighthood: wisdom, loyalty, freedom, oneness, character, love (Appendix B).

HEROINEHOOD

My daughter also could have had a sword. However, she felt another symbol was more fitting for her. The symbol my daughter and I chose together was a bow and arrows. Again, I had one custom-made. It also has the family crest and the defining characteristics of heroinehood embossed on it: wisdom, loyalty, freedom, oneness, character, love (Appendix B).

POST-KNIGHTHOOD/HEROINEHOOD

With the initiation journey complete, your children have been ushered into adulthood. The joy of that journey, all coming together in that sacred moment, is beyond words. There is something purely divine in telling your son or daughter that the time has come for them to stand as a man or woman. They are adults, and you have shared an incredible journey to lead them there.

But being adults does not mean they no longer need you! Yes, things are different as you stand arm in arm with your now adult children. However, they are *inexperienced* adults. You have spent years building a strong, open, trusting relationship with your children. They will continue to lean on you as they move out of the home, join the military, work, go to college, get an apartment, date, marry, start careers, have kids of their own, buy a home . . .

In other words, you will always be their dad, and your fatherhood journey is hardly over. But you also know that they have been prepared and "trained to overcome all things." They are deeply rooted in their sacred identity as beloved sons and daughters and have everything they need for their lives with God—and for a lifetime with you in shared apprenticeship with Jesus.

FINAL THOUGHTS

It is likely that some of you reading this have different circumstances. In other words, not all of you have young children who have not yet turned 8 or 9. I want to encourage you by reminding you of a couple things. First, I'll go back to the beginning to highlight, again, how all of this unfolded for us. I had awakened to and was inspired by the idea of initiation. I went in search of a model I could reimagine for me and my family. The knighthood model resonated with me, and my kids were at an age that fit with the ten-year journey I had reimagined.

However, had they been older, it wouldn't have stopped me. I would have prayerfully continued the work of imagining how I might make some adjustments that would work for us anyway. The knighthood model we used is not a sacred cow. It is a framework to carry the vision for your family to help them understand and receive the intentionality you are ready to offer. You are awakened to the promise of fatherhood, and you are now beginning to see clearly how to embrace and fulfill that promise.

Our model may not quite fit you and your family. That's okay. Reimagine, as I did, and God will guide you into a way forward that works for your family. As a reminder, if you are interested in support for discovering what this might look like for you and your family, more individualized opportunities and resources can be found through theintentionaldad.org .

Appendix B

SYMBOLISM

The ceremonies of initiation are essential in sealing key milestone moments of the initiation journey. Just as important, though, is the rich tradition-worthy symbolism that accompanies the ceremony. These are the symbols we used to seal the milestone moments. For those reading the print version, scan the QR code at the end of the appendix to see these images in color.

PAGEHOOD: FAMILY CREST

The armor and sword represent the life of a warrior knight/warrior heroine that God has designed for each of his beloved sons and daughters to live. The symbols on the crest represent each element that together reveal the vision for the life Jesus lived and, therefore, the life God is growing us up for as well.

- Lamp: Guided by wisdom

- Ring: Uncompromising in loyalty

- Eagle: Inspired by freedom

- Grail: Motivated by oneness

- Treasure Chest: Firm in character

- Heart on Fire: Driven by love

The Latin at the bottom translates: "For the King"—a reminder of our purpose of being kingdom bearers bringing the kingdom wherever we go as we live our lives as his apprentices and ambassadors.

The colors also are significant:

- Silver/White: Signifies truth, sincerity, peace, innocence, and purity
- Gold: Signifies wisdom, generosity, glory, constancy, and faith
- Blue: Signifies loyalty, chastity, truth, strength, and faith
- Red: Signifies magnanimity, strength with honor, power with self-control

SQUIREHOOD: SHIELD

The shield is steel and is custom-painted with the crest. It symbolizes the age of responsibility as these are the years that the child grows in responsibility and skills in guarding their hearts and living their lives of apprenticeship with Jesus.

KNIGHTHOOD: SWORD

The symbol for the knighthood ceremony is a sword. I had one custom made with wisdom, loyalty, and freedom engraved on one side of the blade and oneness, character, and love engraved on the other. The family name is engraved at the base of the sword on one side, and *Pro Rex* is on the other. The handle is wrapped in blue and red leather with gold accents to match the colors of our crest.

HEROINEHOOD: BOW AND ARROWS

At the time of the writing of this book, Ellie's initiation ceremony has not yet happened. But we are already preparing for the moment. She could have had a sword but, together, we decided that a bow and arrows would be a wonderful fit for her personality and, therefore, a fitting way to differentiate her ceremony from her brother's. The crest is painted on the grip. Wisdom, loyalty, and freedom are embossed on the upper arm while oneness, character, and love are embossed on the lower. The arrows are red, blue, white, and gold to match the colors of our crest.

Scan to view images in color.

Appendix C

SCRIPTURE FOR FURTHER EXPLORATION

Supplemental to Chapters 7 and 8 (Identity),
9 (Vision), and 10 (Purpose)

IDENTITY

WHAT IS TRUE:
Jeremiah 4:22
Isaiah 29:13
Romans 3:10-18

WHAT HAPPENED?
Genesis 2:15-17, Genesis 3:5-6

WHAT IS MOST TRUE:
John 3:16
Isaiah 53
John 15:13
Galatians 3:26-29

John 1:12-13
Psalm 18:19
Romans 8:14-17
Jeremiah 31:33
Psalm 139
Luke 12:7
Genesis 1:31
Matthew 5:14-16
Acts 4:13
Psalm 8:3-8
Romans 8:31-39

It is true that I am broken and have missed the mark as a sinner. My failure is real and God most certainly does not ignore it. But that is only part of the story. There is much more. What is most true is that I am a beloved son/daughter of God. I am loved. I belong. I have nothing to prove.

VISION

FIRM IN CHARACTER
Proverbs 8:1-36
Proverbs 9:1-18

UNCOMPROMISING IN LOYALTY
Daniel 3:1-30
James 1:2-4
Romans 5:3-5
Romans 8:28-29

And these verses that model authenticity with God in the midst of suffering:

Psalm 22:1-21 Honesty, Authenticity
Psalm 22:22-31 Unshakable trust
Psalm 38:1-20 Honesty, Authenticity
Psalm 38:21-22 Hopeful trust

INSPIRED BY FREEDOM

Consider what each of these verses reveals about what we're freed from and simultaneously freed for. Remember, biblical freedom is distinct from concepts of freedom Westerners (especially Americans) hold. True freedom is not "getting to do whatever I want." Instead, true freedom comes as we live more fully according to God's design.

Galatians 5:1-6
John 8:31-36
Romans 8:31-39
Ephesians 4:22-24
Matthew 18:21-22
Proverbs 29:18
Luke 4:18-19
Isaiah 41:10
Matthew 10:42
Acts 2:44
Galatians 3:26-29

MOTIVATED BY ONENESS

Genesis 1-3. This was discussed a lot in the book. Explore the original design and, again, look at what the enemy did with Eve and Adam. The lies are intended to separate us from God. Jesus tells us the design is to remain in him:
John 15:1-10
If we are to remain in Jesus, we must respond to those two lies.
Mark 12:30
Romans 8:38-39

Matthew 23 for Jesus' scathing assessment of Pharisees missing God's desire for oneness

John 10:1-5

FIRM IN CHARACTER

Romans 5:1-5

2 Peter 1:3-9

Galatians 5:22-23

DRIVEN BY LOVE

Philippians 2:1-11

John 13:34-35

Matthew 22:36-40

1 Corinthians 13:1-13

PURPOSE

THE STORY WE LIVE IN:

Genesis 1-3

Isaiah 53

John 3:16

Luke 15

THE WAR AND OUR ENEMY:

Ephesians 6:10-12

THE WAR AND OUR MISSION:

Proverbs 4:23

2 Corinthians 5:20

Matthew 22:36-40

ABOUT THE AUTHOR

Aric is founder of The Intentional Dad, a ministry dedicated to awakening, encouraging, equipping, and anointing men for the sacred calling of fatherhood. He is an author, teacher, fatherhood coach, and spiritual counselor who is passionate about shepherding men and their families on the journey to gain the skills and heart to embrace and fulfill the promise of fatherhood. Aric lives in Michigan, is a father of three, and has been married to his best friend, Mary Jo, for twenty-nine years. He has a Master's degree in Theological Studies, taught elementary age kids (pre-K through second grade) for five years, and offers more than two decades of experience as a father and, especially, his family's experiences in living out a vision for a ten-year initiation process for his sons and daughter. He invites men and their families to set out on their own journey and share in the indescribable joy of being an intentional dad.

ACKNOWLEDGMENTS

As I take a few moments to reflect on this journey, I can't help but feel a little nostalgic . . . and also very grateful. I am thanking God for the people he has put in my life with the wisdom, encouragement, challenging words, and loving support I needed exactly when I needed it.

Dad, our journey together has seen more than its fair share of twists and turns. In writing this book, I knew I would be sharing some challenging parts of our story. I love and respect you too much to do that without first inviting you into the writing process, but I wasn't sure how you would feel about it. You accepted my invitation anyway. What unfolded for us was a gift that overwhelms me with deep, deep gratitude. God had something far more precious in store for us as we received healing and reconciliation that has been straight from his heart. You have been a source of profound encouragement that only a father can give. I love you, Papa. I am so proud to call you Dad!

For my bride, my best friend, and the woman with whom I share this adventure of parenthood. Mary Jo, I look back on the life we've built and gratitude overwhelms me. You have saturated our twenty-nine years with unshakable belief, encouragement, and selfless support. It was no different with this book. I couldn't have done this without you. "Thank you" hardly seems like it's enough for the woman who is my soulmate and inspiration. I love you, honey.

Only three people call me by the precious name Dad. Living into a ten-year journey has been rewarding and, let's be honest, also very difficult at times. Ben, Ellie, and Ian, what we have shared has been far from perfect, but it has all been worth it. You are the reason I have a fatherhood story to tell. Thank you for your willingness to take this epic journey with me, for trusting me, for forgiving me when I let you down, for the courage to keep going and, most importantly, for simply being my children. I am so proud of each of you and eternally grateful for the privilege and honor of being your Dad.

To my brothers, Ryan, Tyler, and Paxton, thank you for your encouragement, support, and love not just for this book but for being there for us through all the twists and turns through the years. And Tyler, thank you for the hours spent walking through drafts, encouraging me when I was overwhelmed, challenging me when you knew I could do better, and thinking with me when I needed someone to sharpen me.

To my spiritual father, Pete, thank you for the encouragement and wisdom you have poured into me all these years. You are indeed a "rescuer of men's hearts." I am one of so very many.

Mark and Matt, your coaching and counsel have helped me walk the long road back into vocational ministry. You have encouraged me and helped me gain clarity for what I have to offer through The Intentional Dad.

Gabe and Lindsey, you have encouraged and sharpened me. Our experiences together have been an important part of this book, and your friendship has been a true blessing to me and my family.

Finally, thank you to my brothers in True Pursuit and the men who meet every Wednesday night. It is a true blessing to have a community of men that knows how to fight for one another, who share in the strength of vulnerability, and who inspire one another to live ever more deeply from our belovedness. You have offered love and belonging to a man who needed (and still needs) lots of healing around community. I am so grateful for your hearts, authenticity, and encouragement.

No story is lived in a vacuum. I am no different from anybody else in that my story is the culmination of life lived with and among people who have influenced, known, loved, and challenged me. I am so grateful for all of you, and I can't wait to see what God does next.

NOTES

PROLOGUE

1. Merriam-Webster.com Dictionary, s.v. "submit," accessed July 29, 2022, https://www.merriam-webster.com/dictionary/submit.

2. Merriam-Webster.com Thesaurus, s.v. "submit," accessed July 29, 2022, https://www.merriam-webster.com/thesaurus/submit.

CHAPTER ONE: THE PROMISE OF FATHERHOOD

1. "The Consequences of Fatherlessness," fathers.com, https://fathers.com/statistics-and-research/the-consequences-of-fatherlessness/2/.

CHAPTER THREE: INITIATION: THE ANCIENT WISDOM OF INTENTIONAL FATHERHOOD

1. Brennan Manning, *Abba's Child: The Cry of the Heart for Intimate Belonging* (Colorado Springs: NavPress, 2002), p. 51.

2. Henri Nouwen, *Spiritual Direction: Wisdom for the Long Walk of Faith* (New York: Harper Collins, 2006), pp. 28-29.

CHAPTER FOUR: THE MATRIX

1. The Wachowski Brothers, dir. *The Matrix*. Burbank, CA: Warner Bros. Entertainment, 1999.

2. C.S. Lewis, *Mere Christianity* (New York: Touchstone, 1996), p. 51.

3. C.S. Lewis, *The Screwtape Letters* (New York: Harper Collins, 1996), ix.

4. Nouwen, pp. 28-29.

CHAPTER FIVE: AND SO IT BEGINS

1. John Eldredge, *Wild At Heart: Discovering the Secret of a Man's Soul* (Nashville: Thomas Nelson Publishers, 2001), p. 106.

2. Peter Jackson, dir. *The Lord of the Rings: The Two Towers*. Burbank, CA: Warner Bros. Entertainment, 2002.

CHAPTER SIX: CRITICAL WEAKNESS

1. Manning, p. 64.

2. John Eldredge, *Waking the Dead: The Glory of a Heart Fully Alive* (Nashville: Thomas Nelson Publishers, 2003), p. 152.

CHAPTER SEVEN: JUST WHO DO YOU THINK YOU ARE?

1. Frank Darabont, dir. *The Shawshank Redemption*. Burbank, CA: Warner Bros. Entertainment, 1994.

2. John Eldredge, *Get Your Life Back: Everyday Practices for a World Gone Mad* (Kindle Version) (Nashville: Nelson Books, 2020), chapter 8.

3. Brennan Manning, *The Ragamuffin Gospel* (New York: Multnomah, 2005), pp. 13, 14.

CHAPTER EIGHT: INVITATION

1. Peter Scazzero, *Emotionally Healthy Spirituality: It's Impossible to Be Spiritually Mature While Remaining Emotionally Immature* (Grand Rapids: Zondervan, 2017), p. 114.

2. Eldredge, *Wild At Heart*, p. 106.

3. Elizabeth Kubler-Ross and David Kessler, *On Grief and Grieving: Finding the Meaning of Grief Through the Five Stages of Loss* (New York: Scribner, 2014).

4. Richard Rohr, *Adam's Return: The Five Promises of Male Initiation* (Kindle Edition) (New York: The Crossroad Publishing Company, 2004), ch. 9.

5. J. Dwight Pentecost, *The Parables of Jesus: Lessons in Life from the Master Teacher* (Grand Rapids: Kregel Publications, 1998), p. 61.

CHAPTER NINE: VISION

1. Andy Stanley, "The Best Question Ever," YouTube, July 24, 2012, educational audio recording, 2:10-2:34, https://youtu.be/dCVsocDVsxY .

2. Andrew Adamson, dir. *The Chronicles of Narnia: The Lion, the Witch, and the Wardrobe.* Burbank, CA: Buena Vista Home Entertainment, 2006.

3. John Mark Comer, *Live No Lies: Recognize and Resist the Three Enemies That Sabotage Your Peace* (Colorado Springs: Waterbrook, 2021), p. 231.

4. Dallas Willard, *The Great Omission: Reclaiming Jesus' Essential Teachings on Discipleship* (Kindle Edition) (New York: Harper Collins, 2006), ch. 6.

5. John Eldredge *Get Your Life Back,* ch. 8.

CHAPTER TEN: PURPOSE

1. Jackson, *The Lord of the Rings.*

APPENDIX A: KNIGHTHOOD MODEL FOR INITIATION

1. Robert Lewis, *Raising a Modern-Day Knight: A Father's Role in Guiding His Son to Authentic Manhood* (Wheaton: Tyndale House Publishers, 1997), pp. 16-17.